MACROECONOMICS

CASES AND SCENARIOS

Learn Economics via Cases and Scenarios

ELIJAH M. JAMES, PH. D.

Canadian Cataloguing in Publication Data

James, Elijah M.

Macroeconomics Cases and Scenarios

ISBN 978-1-7383576-2-8

EJ Publishing

663 White Hills Run

Hammonds Plains

Nova Scotia, Canada B4B 1W7

Lovingly dedicated to the memory
of the late Tommy Ephraim from whom
I learned much in the school of life

TABLE OF CONTENTS

PREFACE

Brief Description

This book, consisting of 75 cases and scenarios, is designed to give students a more comprehensive grasp of economics. The advantages of the case method are well documented. The cases and scenarios that comprise this book place the student in *possible* economic situations where he or she learns not just economic jargon and theory but is also given opportunities to apply theory in providing solutions to possibly real economic problems. Economics comes to life in the various cases and scenarios provided, and very importantly, students perceive the importance of economics in their own lives, present and future. Every effort is made to ensure that the student is deeply involved with the material and that a high level of interest is maintained throughout.

Macroeconomics: Cases and Scenarios is intended primarily for students taking courses in introduction to macroeconomics, but students taking intermediate macroeconomics will also find the book to be very useful. The book is intended to be supplementary to a main textbook on macroeconomic principles.

Outstanding Features

The following are some of the outstanding features of *Macroeconomics: Cases and Scenarios:*

- Highly interactive and student-centered
- A novel and effective use of cases and scenarios to learn economics
- Verbal skills, critical thinking skills, and analytical skills are developed

- The approach emphasizes the relevance of economics in students' lives
- Visual aids (graphs) are used extensively
- Designed to be used in any English-speaking country
- Unparalleled for help with test and exam preparation.

A concerted effort has been made to bring analysis to bear on real problems. All answers are purported to be written by the student reading the cases and scenarios through the performance of assigned tasks in various situations. Thus, the student is fully integrated into the learning process.

Pedagogical Features

There is no shortage of pedagogical features in this book.

Tasks

At the end of each case or scenario, the student is asked to perform a specific task. The performance of that task helps the student to develop written communication, critical thinking, problem-solving, and analytical skills. At the same time, the student learns how to apply macroeconomic theory to the design of macroeconomic policy.

Pictures

Pictures are used extensively throughout the book to create the mood and to set the stage for the scenarios. Pictures are used in this book in much the same way as music is used in films. They create a relationship with the scenario, create the appropriate atmosphere, evoke desired emotions, and add a sense of reality to the cases and scenarios. They take the student from where he or she is to where the author would like her or him to be.

Humour

Humour is used liberally to capture and maintain the student's interest. Other pedagogical advantages of humour are: the enhancement of the learning environment and hence learning outcomes, a higher retention rate, and the reduction of anxiety, all of which are conducive to learning.

Sample Tests

An entire section of this book (Part 7) is devoted to sample tests. It includes six sample tests on the material typically covered in a course in introductory macroeconomics. Answers are provided so that students can compare their answers with those given. These are pedagogical devices as well as grade boosters.

Other pedagogical tools

A wide variety of other pedagogical tools are used throughout the book. The cases and scenarios consist, for example, of dialogues, lectures, radio and TV shows, picnic, conversations, internet searches, study groups, conventions, travel, games, and, believe it or not, even dreams.

Level

The book is intended for undergraduate students taking courses in introductory macroeconomics. The book does not assume any prior knowledge of the subject on the part of the student. Students taking intermediate macroeconomics will also find the book of immense value.

The Competition

Although the idea of using cases and scenarios in economics is not new, the nature of the cases and scenarios and how they are used in this book are unique. In my research, I have not been able to find a book that is similar to *Macroeconomics: Cases and Scenarios*. I am not aware of any similar works completed or in progress. In general, the book will compete in the market with other learning guides and alternative formats, but I know of no close substitutes for *Macroeconomics: Cases and Scenarios*.

Acknowledgements

My indebtedness to friends, colleagues, teachers, and students seems to multiply with every book I write. When I decided to write this book, I discussed the idea with several people, all of whom gave their enthusiastic endorsements.

I am extremely grateful to many of my students at Dawson College who willingly agreed to use some of the scenarios. Their comments significantly improve the effectiveness of the book.

It would be remiss of me if I did not single out my friend and colleague, Dr. Alaka Ganguli, who strongly encouraged the use of cases and scenarios in the teaching of economics. Thank you, Alaka, you have been an inspiration.

Finally, to my children, Ted and Andrea, thank you for your unflinching support of my work all through the years.

I thank you all.

Elijah M. James

PART I

INTRODUCTION

Scenario 1: Hiring an Economist

You are employed as a Human Resources Officer at the Large Variety Corporation (LVC)—a fictitious company that produces and sells a large variety of household items such as electric fans, kitchen utensils, clocks, reading lamps, vacuum cleaners, etc. At its last board meeting, the company discussed the possibility of hiring an economist. Knowing that you have studied economics, the Human Resources Manager has asked you to prepare a document detailing why it would be a good idea to hire an economist for her to include in her presentation at the next board meeting.

Task

Your task is to prepare a 250-word report for the Human Resources Manager explaining convincingly why it would be advantageous for LVC to hire an economist.

Scenario 2: What Exactly do Economists do?

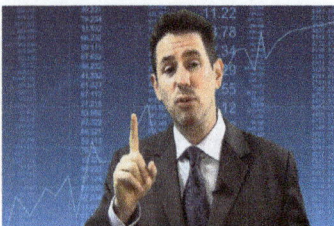

At a meeting of the Board of Directors of the NOW Corporation, there was a lively discussion regarding employing an economist. After listening to various arguments, the Board decided to employ the services of an economist on a full-time basis because its main competitors have hired economists and they seem to be prospering as a result. The Human Resources Manager has to prepare a job description for the economist's position and has called upon you to draft such a job description.

Task

You are required to draft the job description so that the Human Resources Department can post the job. Your description must show that you know what economists do.

Scenario 3: Economic Growth—A Controversial Issue? Applying Economic Reasoning

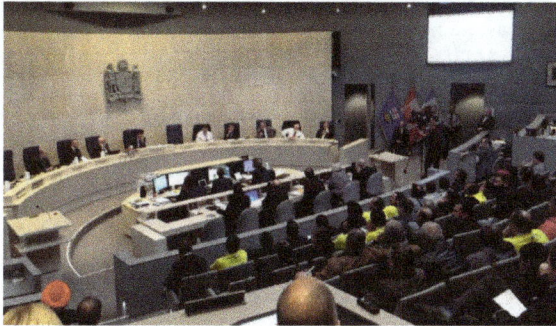

At a city hall meeting in Econoville (an imaginary city), there is a heated debate about the effects of economic growth. One group extols the virtues of economic growth while the other denounces the evils of more economic growth. The outcome of this debate is crucial for the decision that the city has to make regarding its tangible support (or lack of it) for more economic growth.

The supporters of more economic growth claim that had it not been for economic growth, the standard of living in Econoville would not be anywhere close to where it is now. Economic growth must be credited with educational opportunities now easily available, with a health care system that is the envy of many, and with Econoville's ability to provide the high level of services offered to its residents— excellent garbage collection, well-paved and properly maintained streets, numerous parks, adequate housing, etc. They maintain that the pursuit of economic growth is mandatory if Econoville is to be able to maintain or improve the well-being of its residents.

The detractors of more economic growth emphasize the view that although economic growth enables residents to purchase bigger and more beautiful homes, buy bigger and more luxurious cars, take more vacations to exotic places, and enjoy all the amenities that Econoville is able to provide, these are only *physical things* and they do not guarantee happiness. Moreover, they claim, economic growth comes at the expense of more traffic congestion, greater environmental degradation, and increased emotional stress that take a toll on our health and wellness. They maintain that more economic growth is not worth the cost.

Task

Your task is to apply the economic way of thinking to this controversial issue so that the city can make an informed choice.

Scenario 4: Economics, a Science? Never!

Imagine that you have come across the following article in a magazine:

The great advances that have been made in science have inspired such confidence in anything scientific that many disciplines are finding ways to classify themselves as sciences. It is well known that fields of study such as physics, chemistry, biology, and botany are sciences. In such fields of study, observation, measurement, and experimentation in laboratories are what make them sciences. I heard someone talking about *economic science* the other day and I could hardly believe my ears. The speaker was trying to make the point that economics was a science. I said to myself: "What! Economics a science? It can never be." Economists do nothing but philosophize on certain aspects of the economy.

If economics can claim to be a science, then dog catchers are scientists.

Nilton Freeman (Fictitious)

Task

As a student of economics, you are to write a letter to Mr. Freeman, defending the right of economics to be considered a science.

Scenario 5: Why don't they listen? Economists as Advisers

leaders
who don't listen
will eventually
be surrounded
by people who
have nothing to say

Andy Stanley

The ruling party of a particular country hired two economic advisers at very attractive salaries to advise the Prime Minister on economic matters. The role of the economic advisers is stated specifically as follows: "To study the impact of government policies on the economy and to advise the Prime Minister accordingly." Six months after the employment of the economic advisers, one of them was heard saying: "I am so frustrated in this job. We have done an excellent job of analyzing the effects of government policies, and the Prime Minister has openly expressed his total satisfaction with our work. Yet he has not followed our advice." Why don't these leaders listen to the advice of their advisers?"

Task

Your task is to answer the question posed in this scenario. Why don't they listen?

Scenario 6: Economists at the Picnic: Disagreement Among Economists

The members of the Department of Economics at Athelma University (fictitious) went on a picnic. As might be expected, they started to debate different aspects of the economy. The discussion began with Dan asking Paul whether he had come to accept the wisdom of imposing a tax on cigarettes. Paul responded that he remained firm in his position that the tax was just another example of a tax grab to stuff the government's coffers. Paul then asked Jim, who was sitting opposite him at the picnic table, if he was still adamant that the reduction in the rate of interest would have only minimal impact on the level of investment. Jim responded that he was at a loss trying to figure out why Paul insisted that the impact on investment would be huge. Betty, Dan's wife, then interrupted with the suggestion that they ate lunch.

Task

Your task is to study the discussion in the scenario and explain why these economists disagreed.

Scenario 7: A Land Flowing with Milk and Honey. Any Scarcity Here?

The following dialogue took place between Miss Green and Mr. Brown on the subject of scarce resources in Jorobel (an imaginary country).

Miss Green: All this talk about scarce resources in Jorobel is getting to me.

Mr. Brown: It's utterly ridiculous. We have an abundance of all kinds of resources in Jorobel.

Miss Green: For sure. We have lots of land, a relatively large and growing population, an abundance of water in the form of rivers and lakes, and deposits of precious metals with which no country can compare.

Mr. Brown: You see; they take this idea of scarcity and try to apply it everywhere. Well, it certainly does not apply to us in Jorobel. Ours is a land flowing with milk and honey. No scarcity here. See you at the party later.

Miss Green: Yes, I'll be there.

Task

Answer the following question on the basis of the dialogue between Miss Green and Mr. Brown.

a) What concept of scarcity might Miss Green and Mr. Brown have in mind when they denied the existence of scarcity in Jorobel?

b) Is there scarcity in Jorobel? How so?

John has recently graduated from university with a degree in economics and is currently employed full-time as a junior economist with Zest Sales (a fictitious marketing company) at an annual salary of $40,000. Before attending university, John worked as a sales representative at a salary of $30,000. While attending university, he had to live away from home. The following information about the annual cost of attending university is available:

Tuition	$12,000
Other fees	2,500
Room	6,500
Meals	5,500
Books	1,400
Insurance	1,000
Miscellaneous	600
Total	$29,500

Task

Answer the following questions based on the scenario given:

a) What important cost item is missing from the calculation of John's total cost of attending university?

b) Calculate John's total cost of attending university.

c) If John was unemployed before he decided to attend university because he just could not find a job, what then would be his total cost of attending university?

Scenario 9: Enrolment Planning at a University. Anything to Do With Opportunity Cost?

Best Business University (BBU) – an imaginary private university—is well known for the high quality of its business courses. BBU is not unlike the university shown here.

An administrator from BBU met with the university's economic consultant to discuss plans for enrolment for the next three years. The forecasted unemployment figures for the next five years for the region from which the university draws the vast majority of its students are presented below.

Year	Unemployment rate
1st year	10%
2nd year	15%
3rd year	21%
4th year	16%
5th year	15%

The following conversation is what occurred between the university administrator and the economic consultant:

Admin: Here we are again, planning for enrolment.

Con: Yes. I can't believe it's been an entire year since we met. Time really flies.

Admin: We should have an easy time now though. With the employment situation for the next few years, it is clear that our enrolment will fall significantly. It will be difficult for people to pay school fees. We should shelve the plan to add additional classrooms.

Con: I don't see it that way. I think we should expect an increase in enrolment since more students will be seeking admission. We should actually plan to add additional classrooms.

Admin: What? That is strange.....

Task

Your task is to write a report of about 180 words explaining whose view of the course of enrolment at BBU is correct.

Scenario 10: Calculating Real Profit. The Economist's Approach

Your aunt, Violet, after working at the Bread of Life Bakery and Café (a fictitious business) for seven years, was promoted to Assistant Manager. The owner of the bakery decided to sell the store. It was Violet's dream to own her own bakery, so this, she thought, was a golden opportunity. She bought Bread of Life. It was just a month earlier that she turned down an offer of $60,000 a year to manage a competing bakery.

Violet has often wondered whether or not she had made the right decision by refusing the offer to manage the competing bakery. The income statement for the first year of operation after Violet bought the store is as follows:

Sales	$1,500,000
Direct cost of goods sold	900,000
Gross margin	**600,000**
Operating expense:	
Advertising and promotion	8,000
Payroll expense	170,000
Interest and taxes	120,000
Permits and licenses	500
Miscellaneous	11,000
Total operating expenses	**309,500**
Net profit	**290,500**

Wanting to put as much money as possible back into the business, Violet did not draw a salary for the entire year. She looked at the bottom line and smiled. She had made almost $300,000.

Task

Your task is to review the information provided in the scenario from an economic perspective and prepare a 160-180 word statement so that Violet can know how well Bread of Life has done in its first year of operation under her ownership.

Scenario 11: Presentation for the Park. Explain it with Production-Possibility Curves

The city of Parkland (a fictitious city) has a fixed amount of money (budget) to spend on its recreation parks. A decision is being made as to whether to use the funds to create additional parking spaces or to increase the number of playground equipment. Not surprisingly, people who drive to the parks support the idea of additional parking places while pedestrians tend to support the idea of more playground equipment.

The Director of Parks and Recreation for the city is preparing a presentation for an upcoming town hall meeting. The objective of the presentation is to present different scenarios and explain the possibilities that each scenario offers. In his presentation, he wants to use a set of graphs because he believes that the visual aids will add effectiveness to his presentation. The following are the main points that he wants to illustrate graphically.

a) With its given budget, the city cannot provide more parking spaces *and* more playground equipment at the same time.

b) The city allocates additional funds to the Department of Parks and Recreation with the condition that such funds can be used only to expand the parking areas.

c) Because of a significant increase in the number of families moving to Parkland, the demand for parking spaces increases.

d) Parkland decides to increase the budget of the Department of Parks and Recreation.

Economic Consulting Associates (ECA), your employer, has been given a contract to produce the necessary graphs for the Director of Parks and Recreation.

Task

As a junior economic consultant with the company, you have been given the assignment to produce the series of graphs requested by the Director. Your task is to produce the graphs as requested, in a document containing between 180-200 words, and applying the appropriate economic model.

Scenario 12: Not a Drum was heard for the Free Market System

Assume that you were at a political rally organized by the Socialist Party. Speaker after speaker extolled the virtues of a command economy in which the main factors of production are owned and used by the government. Speaker 1 spoke about the inability of a capitalist system to automatically generate full employment. Speaker 2 spoke about the tendency for certain goods to be under-produced in a free-market economy, and Speaker 3 spoke about the tendency for the environment to be overlooked in a capitalist economy. And on and on they went. A lone, high-pitched voice shouted: "Down with the free-market system." Not a drum was heard for capitalism, and not even a funeral note as the free enterprise system was buried at that rally.

Task

You are a staunch believer in the free market system. You are to prepare a statement of about 250 words in which you explain the main advantages of a market-oriented economic system.

Scenario 13: What is the Question? The Free Market Answers

(Cathy and Eugene are sitting in the cafeteria. They had just finished a class with Professor Query. The following conversation ensued).

Eugene: Professor Query sure asks lots of questions. Did you get that "what, how, and for whom" thing that he was trying to explain?

Cathy: Yea. You didn't get it?

Eugene: Sort of, except for the part when he was talking about how a free enterprise economic system answers the "what" question.

Cathy: Do you understand the "what" question?

Eugene: Oh yes. That part is easy. But I don't understand how the free enterprise system answers the question, and we have to know it because Professor Query says it will be on the test.

Cathy: O.K. Let me explain it to you. It's really not that difficult.

Task

Your task is to play the role of Cathy and explain to Eugene how the free enterprise system answers the "what" question.

Scenario 14: Search and You will Find the Circular Flow Model

One evening, you and your best friend were searching for something on the Internet. After a long search, you finally found what you were looking for. Earlier, you were telling your friend who has never taken an economics course, about your economics class and how much you were enjoying it. That sparked her interest in economics so she suggested that you search for economics just to see what you would find. You agreed. A short time after you began your search, the following diagram popped up.

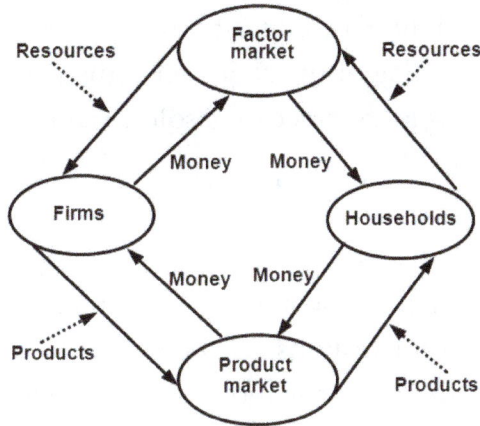

"What is that?" your friend inquired.

Task

Your task is to explain the diagram to your friend.

Scenario 15: Gas Prices—Demand and Supply Can Explain Them

In a city with a population of about 550,000, there are many service stations selling gasoline. It has been observed for the past three years that the price of gasoline fluctuated considerably and quite frequently. Many claim that the fluctuations are due to price-fixing and collusion by the oil companies.

You are employed by a reputable economic consulting firm, Economic Consulting Associates (ECA) as a junior economist. In an attempt to dispel any idea of collusion, an executive of one of the major oil companies has contracted ECA to show that the fluctuations in the price of gasoline can be due to factors other than price-fixing and collusion.

Task

Your supervisor has assigned you the task of preparing a 250-page document demonstrating that price fluctuations can be due to factors other than collusion. Specifically, she wants you to use the model of price determination with graphs in your report.

Scenario 16: Review of Residence Pricing Policy at Best Business University

It has been some time since Best Business University (BBU) revised its residence pricing policy. The university has accommodation for 105 students in its dormitories and currently charges $2,500 per semester per student. The university's housing department is interested in knowing:

a) Whether the university's current residence pricing policy poses a problem.
b) What price change, if any, the university should make.
c) The appropriate rate per semester that the university should charge for accommodation in its dormitories.
d) The effect of an increase in the price of its accommodation on the demand for accommodation at its dormitories.

e) The possible impact on the demand for accommodation at the dormitories at BBU if accommodation at neighbouring residences becomes more expensive.

The university's housing manager is authorized to engage the services of your employer, Economic Consulting Associates (ECA) to analyze the market for housing accommodation at BBU.

The following data on the demand for accommodation at BBU are available.

Price per room/semester ($)	Quantity of rooms demanded/semester
2,800	100
2,700	105
2,600	110
2,500	115
2,400	120
2,300	125
2,200	130

Task

As a junior economist with ECA, you are given the assignment to analyze the market for accommodation at BBU and provide the information required by the housing department in a 150-175 word report.

Scenario 17: Arise and Shine: The Market for Coffee

Violet's Bread of Life Bakery has received a shipment of 2,000 packages of coffee. She intends to price them at $4 per package. A reputable economist has determined that the demand for coffee at Bread of Life is as follows:

Price per package ($)	Quantity demanded
4.50	500
4.00	1,000
3.50	1,500
3.00	2,000
2.50	2,500
2.00	3,000

Remembering your earlier work in reviewing her income statement, Violet has asked your opinion regarding her intention to price the coffee at $4 per package. Specifically, she wants to know:

a) If her intended price of $4 per package will enable her to sell her entire stock, leaving customers not wanting to buy more or less.
b) What price change, if any, she will have to make to enable her to accomplish her objective.
c) The impact of a change in the price of a similar package of coffee at Daily Bread, a competing bakery, on the demand for her product.

Task

You are required to analyze the market for coffee at Bread of Life Bakery and Café and provide the information requested by Violet in a 170-190 word report.

Scenario 18: The Politics and Economics of Minimum Wage Legislation

MINIMUM WAGE
MYTH VS FACT

It's three weeks before the next election and, as usual, the politicians are scrambling for votes. One thing that can be counted on to win votes is the promise of an increase in the minimum wage. This is one of the main planks in the platform of the opposition party. Mr. David Smith (he thinks he is a descendant of Adam

Smith), leader of the ruling party, mused: "Is there any way that I can mount an argument against that minimum wage idea? Oh, I know! I'll ask our economist. Economists usually have a different perspective on such things.

Task

Your task is to prepare an economic analysis of the effects of minimum wage legislation for Mr. Smith so that he can attack the plan of the opposition party.

Scenario 19: Rent Control to the Rescue? A Better Way? The Bare Facts

The city of Pleasantville (a fictitious city) established a Rent Control Board to regulate the rent that landlords can charge their tenants. The objective is to help tenants by preventing rent from rising too fast. Before the institution of rent control, the mayor of Pleasantville used to boast of the beauty of his city with its well-maintained apartment buildings. Ten years after the establishment of the Rent Control Board, slums have begun to appear for the first time in Pleasantville.

Task

Your task is to answer the following questions.

a) Explain how rent control might have contributed to the development of slums in Pleasantville.

b) What alternative step might the city have taken to prevent rent from rising in Pleasantville?

A group of farmers complained that despite huge productivity increases in the farming sector over the years, farmers still earn relatively low incomes while the rest of society benefits from the low price of food. They decided to march to the office of the Minister of Agriculture to protest low farm incomes. Marchers carried placards bearing signs such as those shown here.

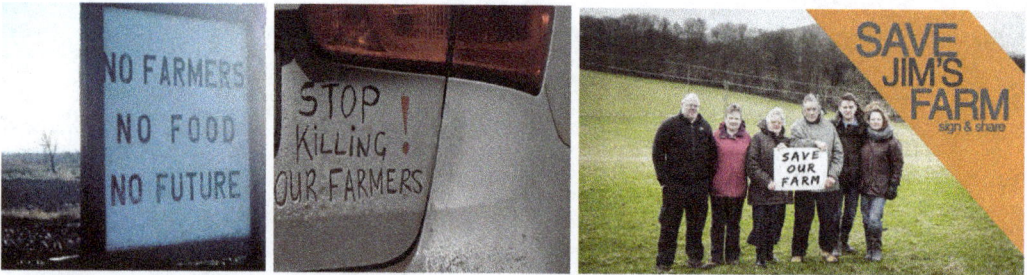

The Minister of Agriculture addressed the farmers, promising that he would immediately address their plight. Shortly thereafter, the government passed a law imposing a quota on the quantity of farm products that farmers can produce.

Task

You are to answer the following questions.

a) Why might farmers not have benefited from increases in their own productivity?
b) Explain how the quota might improve the well-being of farmers.

Scenario 21: Here Comes Professor Noce. Beware of False Demand and Supply Doctrines

Host: Good morning, listeners. Welcome to Radio 101. This morning we are privileged to have Professor Noce with us for the next 30 minutes. Good morning Professor. Welcome.

Professor: Thank you. It's good to be here. Good morning listeners.

Host: Professor, before we begin, I notice that your name, if read from right to left becomes econ, which is often an abbreviation for economics.

Professor: They joke about that all the time in the Economics Department, but it is just a coincidence.

Host: Professor Noce is an economics professor at Nosuch University of Noneconomic Science (NUNS) and he has agreed to answer some questions about economics. Professor, let me begin with this question. We have noticed that the demand for laptop computers has increased significantly over the years. Is this because of a fall in their prices over the years?

Professor: Definitely. There can be no doubt about it. Whenever the price of an item like a laptop computer falls, the demand will always increase. It's what we call the law of demand.

Host: Professor, what will happen to the price of an item when its demand increases?

Professor: Well, we are not sure. You see, when demand increases, the price rises, but when the price rises, the demand decreases which causes the price to fall, so we don't know whether the price will end up being higher or lower.

Host: Very interesting! Professor, a listener wants to know what complementary goods are.

Professor: Well, ahh... My students at Nosuch U often ask this question. Complementary goods are goods that make the user feel proud or gratified. For example, an expensive outfit that makes you feel really good when you wear it is a complementary good. All luxury items such as diamonds, yachts, Rolex watches, and Gucci leather bags are called complementary goods.

Host: People often talk about supply and demand simultaneously as if they are inseparable. How are they related?

Professor: That's a good question. I emphasize this relationship in my classes at NUNS. Whenever demand increases, supply will also increase; and whenever supply increases, demand will also increase. That shows how closely related they are.

Host: Thank you, Professor. You have certainly enlightened us. It's always a pleasure to have you on our show. I look forward to having you again.

Professor: Thank you very much. It was a pleasure.

Task

After studying Professor Noce's responses, you are to indicate any errors in his responses and correct them.

Scenario 22: Sally's Dilemma—Math to the Rescue

Your cousin, Sally, never saw the use of mathematics in high school and often claimed that it was just a waste of time. After graduating from high school, Sally spent two years in the Young Entrepreneur Program at college, after which, she opened Boutique Sally, a classy store in the City Mall. Sally has ordered 100 small bags and would like to know what price she should charge to just clear the market for her bags. She was told that the demand for her bags per month was given by the following equation:

$$Qd = 130 - 3P$$

What does that mean? Sally wondered. She was overheard saying that she wished she had paid more attention to mathematics in school.

Because of successful advertising, the demand for Sally's bags increased by 15 for the next month. Her monthly order has remained at 100 bags and again, she wants to price them so that she has neither a shortage nor a surplus.

Task

You are to use the information provided in this scenario to determine the price that Sally should charge for her bags so that she will have the relevant information.

PART II

NATIONAL INCOME AND EMPLOYMENT

After hearing about the land flowing with milk and honey, you decided to visit Jorobel. Upon your arrival, you were greeted by a friend who held a high position in the government and who informed you that the only economist in the country had recently resigned and had left the country. However, she had left a set of data in the form of tables. Your friend showed you the following two tables:

Table 1 Data for Jorobel

	$million
Consumption expenditure (c)	800
Profits (π)	120
Gross investment (I)	420
Rental income (R)	250
Government purchases (G)	300
Imports (M)	140
Wages (W)	1,100
Exports (X)	160
Interest and dividends (i)	70

Table 2 Data for Petilonia

	(millions of dollars)
Personal expenditure on consumer goods and services (C)	240
Corporate profits before taxes (π)	20
Rental income of persons (R)	10
Income of entrepreneurs (π)	30
Net investment (I_N)	30
Wages and salaries (W)	200
Indirect business taxes (T_{IB})	20
Imports (M)	5
Exports (X)	6
Interest and dividends (i)	60
Depreciation/Capital consumption allowance (D)	40

Your friend, knowing that you are a student of economics with special interest in macroeconomics, asked whether you could use the data for Jorobel to determine its GDP.

Petilonia is a much smaller country than Jorobel, and both countries are currently holding talks with the objective of forming some kind of economic alliance. Your friend asked whether you could take a look at the data for Petilonia and figure out its GDP and particularly how much the government of Petilonia is spending in purchasing goods and services. Without hesitation, you complied with your friend's request.

Task

You are to use Table 1 to compute Jorobel's GDP using the income method and the expenditure method. Also, you are to use Table 2 to calculate Petilonia's GDP and Government purchases of goods and services so that your friend will have the information she needs.

Scenario 24: Where are the Jobs?

It's a Wednesday morning and Jack and Jill are enjoying their 30-minute drive to work. Jill is talking to Jack about a project she is working on, and telling him how much she enjoys working at the Mode Corporation (fictitious). They come to a red light and while they are waiting for the light to change to green, they notice a line of unemployed workers across the street not unlike the one seen below.

Jack comments on how difficult it must be to be out of a job. Jill responds with the question: Why can't the economy provide jobs for these people? After all, they are ready and willing to work.

Task

Your task is to explain why unemployment exists.

Scenario 25: Unemployment is Costly

Okunia (an imaginary country) has been struggling with unemployment for several years. The government has implemented policies and programs to solve the problem but the unemployment rate has remained unacceptably high. The government is particularly concerned with the economic cost of unemployment. The following information is available for Okunia:

GDP = $115 billion

Cyclical unemployment = 9.4%

Task

You are required to use Okun's law to estimate the economic costs of unemployment in Okunia.

Scenario 26: The Varieties of Unemployment

The Department of Labour in Laboria (a fictitious country) believes that labour is the most important resource. A significant portion of its budget is spent on disseminating information about unemployment. A visit to any of its many offices across the country reveals the presence of many leaflets and pamphlets providing information on different aspects of the labour market. Conspicuously absent, however, is any information regarding the different types of unemployment. In an effort to rectify this deficiency, the Director of the Labour Department decided to write a pamphlet explaining the various types of unemployment. She believes that understanding the various types of unemployment will help policymakers to deal more effectively with the problem of unemployment, while at the same time providing useful information to the public. As an employee of the Department of Labour, you are charged with the responsibility of preparing the pamphlet.

Task

Prepare the pamphlet in a document of about 450 words.

Scenario 27: Recover Lost Labour Market Data

You bought a particular issue of a newspaper because it contained labour market data for the first four months of the year in which you are particularly interested. The paper accidentally got wet and some of the data were unreadable. The following are the data that remained:

	January	February	March	April
Adult population	200	200	220	220
Not in labour force	80		90	90
Labour force		110		
Employed	100			
Unemployed		10	30	20
Unemployment rate (%)				
Labour force participation rate (%)				

Task

Use your knowledge of labour-market statistics to recover the lost data.

Scenario 28: The *Real* Crux of the Matter at Fairlee. Don't Forget the Cost of Living

After negotiations between management and the union at Fairlee Manufacturing Plant (FMP) failed to produce a collective agreement, the union decided to stage an unlimited strike.

The company is offering a 4% increase in wages and salaries across the board, but the union contends that the offer is an insult because the rate of inflation is estimated to be 6%. You are a member of the union and, at a union meeting, many workers are saying that a 4% increase is good and should be accepted.

Task

Your task, as a union member, is to explain why a 4% increase is not acceptable.

Scenario 29: Will the Real GDP Please Stand Up?

In the country of Battanovia (fictitious, of course) which was established only five years ago, it was observed that the real GDP has fallen each successive year as shown in the following table.

Year	Real GDP ($ mil)
1	1,101.67
2	999.98
3	989.45
4	982.97
5	979.56

At the same time, the population of Battanovia has remained relatively unchanged. The real GDP has fallen by just over 11% from year one to year 5, yet the people in general do have an increasing amount of goods and services over the years.

Task

Your task here is to explain why the official GDP figures may not fully capture the total output of goods and services produced in Battanovia.

Scenario 30: The Reluctant Philosophers. Effects of Inflation

Bob and Tom go to the park every Wednesday to reminisce on times past and to discuss current events. The community refers to them as the two philosophers—a title that they constantly reject, claiming that they are only commentators on life's events. On this particular Wednesday, their topic of choice was inflation. You happened to be standing within earshot of the two venerable gentlemen when the following conversation ensued.

Bob: Have you seen the newly released figures on inflation?

Tom: No. Are they out?

Bob: Yes. They were published this morning and I am very happy indeed.

Tom: Then the rate must be down.

Bob: Oh no. The rate of inflation is up. It's now running at 8% annually and I am delighted.

Tom: How can you be happy about rising prices? This is terrible news.

Bob Tom

Task

You are required to explain how the two reluctant philosophers can have such different views on the effects of inflation. Why might Bob be delighted while Tom was disappointed?

Scenario 31: Not the Boston Tea Party; Some Protection from Inflation

A group of people are assembled on a Sunday afternoon for a tea party.

Over the years, attendance at the annual affair has not declined at all and may have, in fact, increased, indicating that interest in the event has not waned. However, a decline in the amount of food and drinks provided for the party is obvious. A decrease in the number of new dresses and suits customarily worn by patrons of the party is also noticeable. One outspoken patron is convinced that inflation is to be blamed and she is not afraid to voice her opinion. She is emphatic in expressing her view that no one can escape the damaging effects of inflation.

Task

As a student of economics, your task is to explain how one can protect one's self from inflation.

The Five Star Consulting Group provides economic consulting services to governments. Upon graduation from college, you landed a job as a junior economist with Five Star. The consulting group has been awarded a contract to advise the Government of Recessia (a fictitious country) on certain macroeconomic matters. The following information is available for Recessia.

Real GDP	$1506.83 billion
Cyclical unemployment	4.2%

The Government of Recessia wants to know how much output is lost because of the existing unemployment. It also wants to know what fiscal policy measures can be taken to reduce or eliminate this loss. Additionally, Recessia wants to have in place a fiscal policy measure that can be used in case inflation should occur.

Task

Your immediate supervisor, the senior economist, has turned the file over to you. Specifically, she wants you to use the data given above to calculate the economic cost of unemployment in terms of lost output, that is, the GDP gap. Having calculated the GDP gap, you are to devise fiscal policy measures that will reduce or eliminate the gap. Use the AD/AS model to illustrate how your suggested policy will work, assuming that you subscribe to the modern view of how the macroeconomy works. Since the government wants to be prepared for inflationary periods as well, you are to devise fiscal policy measures that the government will be able to use during inflationary times. You are to use the AD/AS model to illustrate how your suggested policy will work to eliminate or reduce an inflationary gap.

Scenario 33: AD/AS? Show Me in Pictures

Assume that you are a graduate student in economics at the University of Ivaness (imaginary) and that you are a teaching assistant (TA) to Professor Bright. The professor is currently lecturing on the AD/AS model and has asked you to prepare AD/AS graphs to show how each of the following events will affect the equilibrium real GDP and the equilibrium price level, other things being equal.

a) Investment spending increases because of optimistic expectations on the part of entrepreneurs following an announcement by the government that the economy is headed for a period of long-term economic growth. The economy is currently operating in the Keynesian rage of the AS curve.

b) Rapid and prolonged increases in the price of oil cause overall production costs of businesses to rise at a time when the economy is operating in the intermediate range of its AS curve.

c) The government conducts a contractionary fiscal policy to reduce or eliminate an inflationary gap.

d) An economy-wide training program that significantly improves the economy's human capital is implemented when the economy is operating in the intermediate range of its AS curve.

e) A measurable increase in consumer wealth occurs when the economy is operating at its potential GDP.

Task

Your task in this scenario is to prepare the AD/AS graphs as Professor Bright has requested.

Scenario 34: Professor Charle A. Tan Lectures on Fiscal Policy

Professor Charle A. Tan, a close associate of Professor Noce from Nosuch University of Noneconomic Science (NUNS) –(see Scenario 21) expounds on how fiscal policy can be used to combat a situation of high unemployment and low output. Below is his lecture.

There can be little doubt that unemployment is a bane on society. Notice that it is often accompanied by low levels of GDP. Now, except for those people who are unemployed simply because they are too lazy to go to work, economists like myself and my good friend Noce, whom you know well, know how to fix the problem. The remedy is called <u>fiscal</u> policy. I know that some of you like to say <u>physical</u> policy, like physical education, but it is <u>fiscal</u> meaning that it has to do with finance and money and such things. That is why the central bank is so heavily involved. First, I define fiscal (remember, not physical) policy. Fiscal policy refers to the manipulation of the money supply and interest rates by the central bank. Whenever interest rates change, you know that the central bank is conducting fiscal policy.

Now that you know what fiscal policy means, let me show you how it can be used to tackle the problem of severe unemployment and low GDP. What the bank can do in terms of fiscal policy is to reduce the money supply. This reduction in the money supply means that interest rates will rise. As interest rates rise, people will save more, thus making more money available for firms to spend. Now firms have more money so they can hire people and produce more goods and services, thus increasing GDP.

In summary, whenever the economy is experiencing severe unemployment and low levels of GDP, the appropriate fiscal policy is for the central bank to reduce the money supply which will increase interest rates, encourage saving, and cause producers to borrow more money to spend on hiring more workers and thus increase the GDP.

At the end of the lecture, someone whispered that Professor Charle A. Tan was nothing but a charlatan.

Task

Your task is to carefully review Professor Charle A. Tan's lecture and point out any inaccuracies you may discover.

Scenario 35: It's a Roller Coaster. No. It's Sea Waves? No. It's the Business Cycle

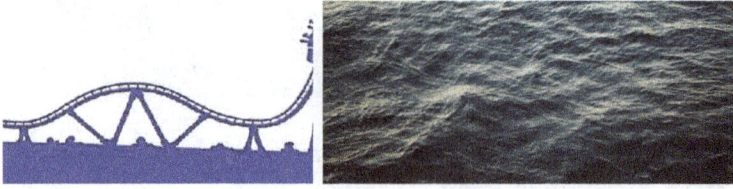

Your macroeconomics professor has just finished a lecture on business cycles. To make sure that you understand the phases of the cycle, she suggested that you explain them to one of your friends who has not taken a course in economics. Great idea! You think. You eagerly rushed off to meet your friend, Sarah. In a vacant classroom, you sat beside her and opened the page in your notebook where the following diagram was drawn.

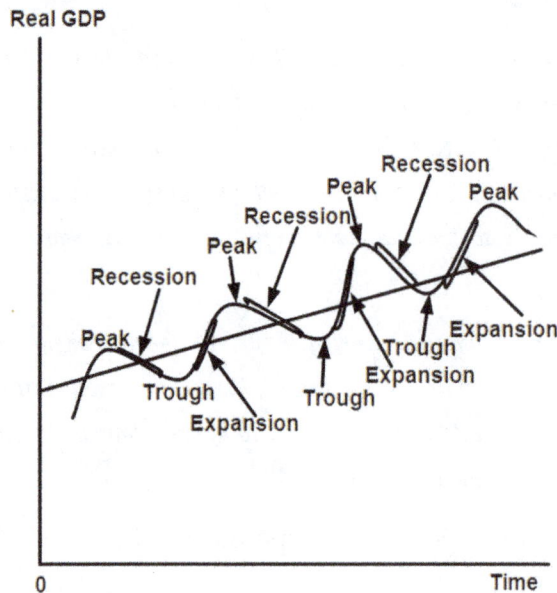

As soon as Sarah saw it, she declared that it was definitely a roller coaster. You smiled pleasantly and assured her that it was not. Then she hazarded a guess that it was sea waves, but she was wrong again.

Task

Your task is to explain the diagram to Sarah as your professor had suggested.

Scenario 36: Study Group in Economics: Sharing the Work on the Business Cycle—Multiplier-Accelerator

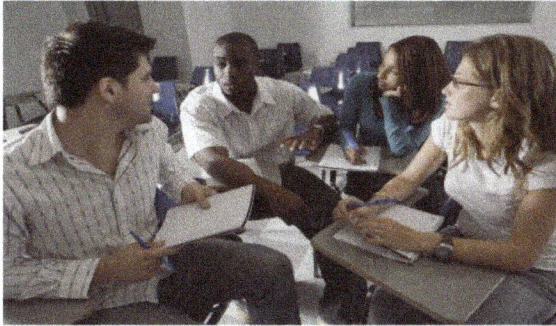

You have known of students forming study groups and you have heard of the benefits of such groups, but you have no personal experience with them because you have never joined one, that is, until now. Your friend, who has a really good grasp of economics, invited you to join a new study group that she was forming. You consented. In class, you were studying the business cycle, so at the first meeting of the group, the group leader suggested that the causes of the business cycle be the topic of discussion at the next meeting. Each group member was assigned a particular task.

Task

Your task was to prepare material on the multiplier-accelerator theory for discussion and distribution at the next group meeting. Go ahead and prepare the material.

Scenario 37: Professor Noce Comments on Unemployment

You probably remember Professor Noce from the economics department at Nosuch University of Noneconomic Science (see Scenario 21). While driving to work, he heard a discussion on the cost of unemployment on Radio 101. With great difficulty, he managed to resist the urge to call the radio station with his own comment. Immediately upon arrival at his office, he called the radio station with the following statement:

"The claim that unemployment results in a loss of income or output is fictitious rather than real; or the claim may be real, but in has no foundation in fact or logic. Let's consider the reality. Why does unemployment exist? The answer is simple. Unemployment exists because people who are willing and able to work just cannot find jobs. Now, it stands to reason that if there are no available jobs, then there can be no loss of income or output attributable to unemployment. The loss of output or income occurs only when jobs are available and people refuse to accept those jobs."

Task

You are required to examine Professor Noce's comment and identify any errors that it may contain.

Scenario 38: You Had a Dream—A Conference of Schools of Thought

You went to bed thinking of the economics test you had early the following morning. You fell asleep before long, and you had the most amazing dream. In that dream, you were at a conference convened to discuss various schools of thought in macroeconomics. In attendance were economists of different persuasions. An official who appeared to be the chairman of the conference was seated at a table with six other distinguished persons, all with microphones in front of them.

After the usual preliminaries, the first person to speak was introduced as Dr. Classical. He looked something like the following photograph. Someone next to me whispered that he was indistinguishable from David Ricardo.

He said that he was there to represent the Classical School that held sway during the 17th and 18th centuries. He explained that their main tenets were the following:

1. Markets are competitive and efficient.
2. All prices, including wages, are flexible.
3. The economy is self-regulating so government intervention is unnecessary if not harmful.
4. The economy achieves full employment automatically.

He concluded by saying that members of his group included Adam Smith, David Ricardo, Thomas Malthus, John Stuart Mill, Jean-Baptiste Say, among others.

Next to speak was Dr. Neoclassical, representing the Neoclassical School. He identified himself as a first cousin of Dr. Classical and claimed that their glory days were the 19th century, but, said he, "We are still very popular today, notwithstanding the 'K' people." He resembled the photo below. A young conference attendant, unable to restrain herself, shouted, "That's Alfred Marshall, I recognize him."

According to Dr. Neoclassical, their main tenets are:

1. Supply and demand determine value.
2. Economic agents are rational.
3. Buyers behave in such a way as to maximize their satisfaction or utility.
4. Producers behave in such a way as to maximize their profits.
5. Competition leads to the efficient allocation of resources.

He was halfway sitting down when he straightened up himself and added proudly that members of his group included William Stanley Jevons, Carl Menger, Leon Walras, Irving Fisher, Alfred Marshall and others. He turned and shook hands with Dr. Classical.

I had no idea who the 'K' people were until the next speaker stood up and introduced herself simply as Dr. K, representing the Keynesian School. There was a loud applause from the audience. From my vantage point, I was able to take the following snapshot of her. Someone remarked that she resembled Joan Robinson.

She noted that her group held fundamentally different views from those held by the Classical and Neoclassical Schools in that they believed that:

1. Changes in total spending (aggregate demand) affect income and employment.
2. The economy can be in equilibrium at less than full employment for a considerable length of time.
3. All prices, including wages, are sticky, especially downward.
4. Active fiscal policy may be necessary to move the economy to full-employment equilibrium.

She mentioned the names of John Maynard Keynes, Joan Robinson, Richard Kahn, John Hicks, Roy F. Harrod, Nicholas Kaldor, John Kenneth Galbraith, Paul Samuelson and a long list of others as belonging to her group. She seemed rather honoured to belong to such a prestigious group.

The next speaker stood to his feet after the chairman announced that he needed no introduction. He did not give his name but the tee-shirt he wore under his jacket bore a big M. He said he represented the Monetarist School. The audience responded with shouts of approval. I was familiar with his facial profile, having seen it on many occasions although I could not remember exactly where or when. He looked a great deal like this:

After the chairman managed to restore order, the speaker continued that the main tenets of the Monetarist School were:

1. Output is variable.
2. The velocity of circulation (the number of times on average that a unit of money is spent per year) varies only slightly.
3. The demand for money varies directly with the price level.

4. Changes in the quantity of money are the major cause of macroeconomic instability.

He paused deliberately and then added,

1. Inflation is always and everywhere a monetary phenomenon.

He identified the following economists as among those belonging to the Monetarist camp: Milton Friedman, Karl Brunner, Phillip Cagan, Alan Meltzer, David Laidler, Anna Schwartz, Alan Greenspan, and Paul Volcker.

It was now time for the next speaker who jumped to his feet and acknowledged that he had a lot in common with Dr. K. In fact, he called himself Dr. New K. and said that he represented the group of economists known as the New Keynesians. I don't recall ever seeing his picture anywhere before, but from memory, he looked like the photo depicted below. Someone beside me whispered that it was Paul Krugman.

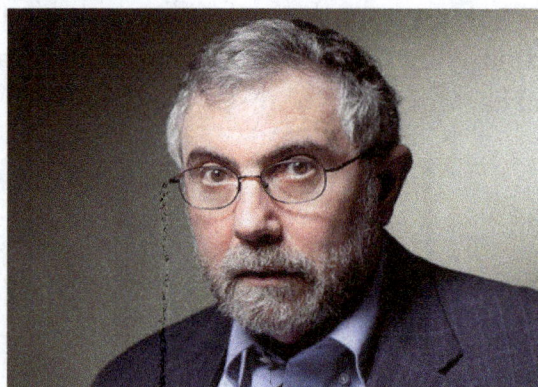

The speaker explained that the New Keynesians believe that:

1. Wages and prices are sticky
2. Markets may not clear quickly
3. Monetary policy has a strong impact on economic activity.

He mentioned that Alan Blinder, Robert J. Gordon, Paul Krugman, Greg Mankiw, Joseph Stiglitz, David Romer, Janet Yellen, and others consider themselves to belong to the New Keynesian School.

The final speaker was Dr. New Classical who thanked Dr. Classical, Dr. Neoclassical, and the representative of the Monetarist School for laying the foundation and paving the way for the New Classical School. Dr. New Classical was vibrant and energetic and looked something like the photo below as he spelled out the main tenets of the New Classical School. The chairman could not resist stating that Dr. New Classical was the spitting image of Stephen Morris. The audience agreed.

Dr. New Classical noted that the main tenets of the New Classical School were:

1. Wages and prices are flexible.
2. Macroeconomic adjustments are swift.
3. Economic agents have rational expectations.
4. If disequilibrium occurs, the economy moves quickly to its natural levels of employment and output.
5. The government need not intervene to achieve full employment.

The chairman of the conference got up to say something when the alarm on my cell phone awoke me. It was then that I realized that it was all a dream.

Task

Reflect on your dream.

Scenario 39: Let the Inventories Speak. Their Role in Output Planning

At a monthly planning meeting of the production department of the Aware Corporation, the following agenda was proposed:

Agenda

1. Adoption of the agenda
2. Minutes of the previous meeting

3. Reports
4. Inventory
5. Next meeting
6. Adjournment

The meeting proceeded smoothly until they came to item #4—Inventory. The chairman spoke at some length about the importance of inventories in signaling the direction of production. He was particularly upset that the report on inventories was not ready at the time of the meeting. According to him, "Our inventories speak to us."

Task

You are to explain why unplanned changes in inventories are so important for the planning process.

Scenario 40: To Be (in equilibrium) or Not to Be? That Is the Question

A little misunderstanding can lead to a big argument. Two students of economics are having a heated argument about an economic issue. Steve insists that in any economy, as long as saving and investment are equal, the economy must be in equilibrium. Emma challenges Steve, telling him that his statement is false. Steve replies that he is surprised that anyone who has taken economics does not know that. The equilibrium condition, he continues, is that saving (S) equals investment (I). Emma points her index finger at him and tells him that he is mistaken.

At this juncture, Steve is adamant that he is right and offers to demonstrate his point. Emma accepts. Steve then pulls out his notebook and turns to a blank page on which he draws the following diagram.

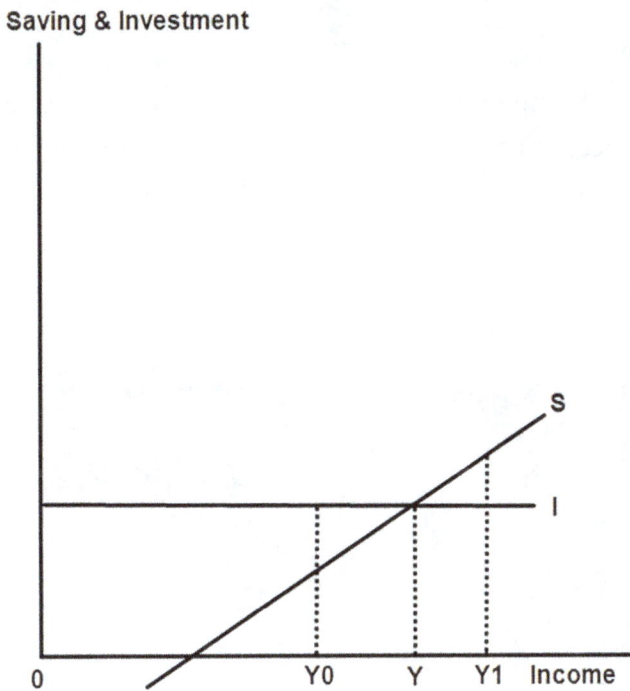

O.K. Steve explains that the curve labelled **I** in the diagram is investment which is assumed not to vary with the level of income, while the curve labelled **S** represents saving which is assumed to increase as income increases. He states that at a level of income above **Y**, such as **Y1**, for example, saving is greater than investment, so the level of income will fall. At a level of income below **Y**, such as **Y0**, investment is greater than saving, so income will rise. However, at a level of income of **Y**, he continues, saving and investment are equal, so the level of income will not change.

That is equilibrium he concludes. He says further that investment is an *injection* of income into the economy while saving is a *withdrawal* of income from the economy, making some reference to some circular flow model. He contends that when they are equal, there must be equilibrium. Feeling rather proud of his presentation, he looks straight at Emma and asks if she is convinced. She looks right back at him and says slowly and deliberately that he is confused and mistaken.

Task

What might Emma have been thinking to cause her to insist that Steve was wrong?

Scenario 41: Algebra Can Help Even When Two Things Seem Different Because Equilibrium Income <u>Is</u> Equilibrium Income, No Matter How It Looks.

Cathy and Eugene (Remember them from Scenario 13?) have been studying together since the beginning of the semester and the partnership has really paid dividends for these two students. In their case, the saying that two heads are better than one is exemplified, or as they say, 'iron sharpens iron.' These two exemplary students are meeting at the university library to discuss (quietly, of course) a lecture just given by Professor Query.

Professor Query had taught that in a closed economy without government, the equilibrium condition $S = I$ was equivalent to $Y = C + I$ where S = saving, I = investment, C = consumer spending and Y = national income or output; and he said that it was a very simple matter to illustrate that fact algebraically. As hard as they tried, neither Cathy nor Eugene could illustrate algebraically that the two equilibrium conditions were identical. In utter frustration they decide to pay a visit to Professor Query's during his office hours.

Task

Your task in this scenario is to illustrate algebraically that S = I and Y = C + I are identical under the given assumptions. Is it as simple as the professor had claimed?

Scenario 42: The Public Debt—The Real Burden

One morning, on your usual commute to school by train, you noticed a newspaper on the vacant seat beside you. Instinctively, you picked it up and started to flip through its pages. On one page was the headline: PUBLIC DEBT BURDENS FUTURE GENERATIONS. It caught your attention because you were studying public debt in your economics class. You began to read the article and it pointed out that the burden of the public debt would be passed on to future generations. As you were reading the article, your mind conjured up the following images of the public debt as explained in the article.

Task

Your task is to point out the misconception about the public debt that is held by the author of the newspaper article.

Scenario 43: Reducing the Deficit

The Government of DeFicitia (a fictitious country) seems to have a chronic deficit problem. A budget deficit is the amount by which government spending exceeds its tax revenues. Year after year, its deficit seems to grow. The government is planning to take measures to reduce its deficit, and on the advice of its economic advisers, it is contemplating reducing government spending or by raising taxes. The government is reluctant to raise taxes because higher taxes tend to make the government unpopular. One economist, who refers to himself as a supply-side economist, suggests that the government can reduce its deficit by reducing taxes.

Task

Explain how it may be possible for a reduction in the tax rate to reduce the deficit.

Scenario 44: Fiscal Policy and the Budget—Quiz for Feedback

Sally is a student at First Choice College (fictitious). She has been studying fiscal policy and the budget for the past week. After each topic, her professor (not Professor Noce of Scenario 21) gives a quiz so that she can evaluate the extent of her understanding of the subject.

Here is the quiz.

1. Matching Items

For each item in Column A, write the letter from Column B that matches the definition. Each letter may <u>not</u> be used more than once. Note that the number of choices in Column B exceeds the number of definitions in Column A.

Column A	Column B
Compulsory payments imposed by a government	Transfer payments
A situation in which government spending equals its revenues	Taxes
The main source of revenue for the federal government	Interventionists
A statement of planned revenues and expenditures	Fiscal policy
Changes in government spending and taxes to achieve desired economic objectives	Budget
A situation in which government spending is less than its revenues	Budget deficit
A school of thought that supports active government involvement in the macroeconomy	Personal income tax
A situation in which government spending is greater than its revenues.	Balanced budget
	Budget surplus

2. Exercise

The following questions refer to the following diagram. G = government spending, T = taxes, and full-employment GDP is $90 billion. Answer the following questions and place your answers in the space provided.

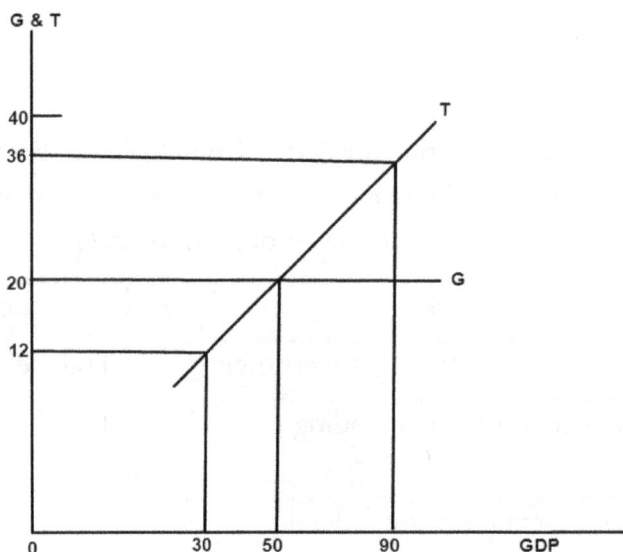

1. How would you describe the full-employment budget?
   a. It has a deficit of $16 billion
   b. It has a deficit of $8 billion
   c. It is in balance
   d. It has a surplus of $16 billion.
2. At what level of GDP is the budget balanced?
   a. $30 billion c. $50 billion
   b. $20 billion d. $90 billion
3. Suppose the economy is at full employment at $90 billion, desired consumption is $50 billion, desired investment is $10 billion and net exports are zero. If full employment is achieved by changing G, leaving taxes unchanged, which of the following should result?
   a. A reduced full-employment surplus
   b. A full-employment deficit
   c. A balanced full-employment budget
   d. None of the above.

Your answers here

Task

Your task is to prepare answers for this quiz for the professor.

Scenario 45: Meeting at the Restaurant—Clarification of Budget Deficit

Thinkecon (not a real company) is a prestigious private economics consulting organization that offers economic advice mainly to governments and large corporations. You have been employed by Thinkecon as an economic adviser mainly in the area of budgetary matters. The Deputy Minister of Finance for the country of Budgetstan (an imaginary country), has approached Thinkecon with a request for a meeting to discuss an assignment related to the budget.

It is a well-known fact that many important decisions, both private and public, are made during meals at restaurants. Some say it's the wine rather than the food. In any event, the Deputy Minister and your boss, the Director of Economics, agreed to meet at a restaurant, not unlike the one pictured below.

For reasons known only to the Deputy Minister and the Minister of Finance, the Deputy wants to be able to show that an increase in the budget deficit does not necessarily mean an increase in overall spending in Budgetstan.

Task

Your boss is preparing a report for the Deputy Minister on budgeting and budgets, and he has asked you to write a short section of about 140 words explaining that an increase in the budget deficit need not mean an increase in overall spending. This section is to be included in his report. Write the section.

Scenario 46: A Balanced Budget May Not Be All Good

(You've just returned home from school and your dad is sitting in his office)

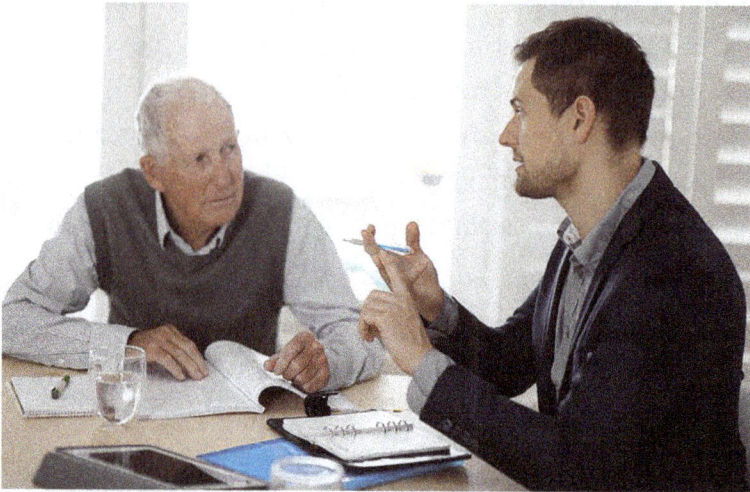

You: Hi Dad!

Father: Hi! How was school today?

You: It was great, especially our economics class.

Father: What did you talk about?

You: It was so interesting. We spoke about the government's budget. You know how you have always said that the government should always balance its budget? Well, I learned today that it may not be always good.

Father: I don't know what kind of economics you are studying, but I know that if the government does not balance its budget, it could be heading for serious trouble. It's just not good to live beyond one's means.

You: Dad, let me explain.

Father: Yes. Go ahead and explain. I can hardly wait.

Task

You are to explain to your father, from an economic perspective, why a balanced budget might not be that desirable.

Scenario 47: What Robin Hood Must Have Accomplished. The Effect of Income Redistribution on Total Consumption

(The following dialogue took place between two friends, Mr. Ambrose and Mr. Benjamin.)

Mr. Ambrose: Good morning Ben. Isn`t it a lovely morning?

Mr. Benjamin: Good morning to you too, Amby. It sure is a beautiful morning. I am sure you've heard of the government's plan to stimulate the economy by significantly increasing taxes on upper-income earners and giving the proceeds to lower-income earners.

Mr. Ambrose: Oh yes. I heard about it. I don't particularly like the idea of paying higher taxes. I don't suppose anyone does, but I don't object to helping lower-income people. However, I really don't see how that policy will help to stimulate the economy.

Mr. Benjamin: I am not quite sure how such things work, but I suppose the government has sought the advice of economists who know about such things.

Mr. Ambrose: Politicians quite often don't follow the advice of their economic advisers. They are more interested in what brings them votes.

Mr. Benjamin: Amby, I see what you mean. There are many more low-income people than there are high-income people, so by taking from the rich and giving to the poor, the government would be making more people happy.

Mr. Ambrose: That's right Ben. It has nothing to do with stimulating the economy. It's just a vote grabber. Think about it Ben. The total amount of money remains the same. It is just distributed differently. That cannot stimulate the economy. The government is just playing Robin Hood to gain popularity.

Mr. Benjamin: It seems as if you are saying that the government is playing Robin Hood in order to be popular with the low-income people. I personally think that the policy will help me because my annual income as a mechanic is less than $30,000. But I can see why a rich lawyer like you, with an annual income of more than $200,000, would oppose the policy.

Mr. Ambrose: My opposition is not to the transfer of income. Ben, you know how much I help the low-income people in this community. My opposition is to the reason the government has given—stimulating the economy. With no extra money, there can be no stimulus.

Mr. Benjamin: O.K., Amby.

Mr. Ambrose: O.K., Ben. See you later.

Task

You are required to explain how a transfer of income, via taxation, from high-income earners like Mr. Ambrose to low-income earners like Mr. Benjamin can stimulate the economy.

Scenario 48: Saving at the Movies

On Tuesday nights at the movies, the tickets are 30% less than on other nights. As to be expected, many moviegoers take advantage of this lower price. It's a Tuesday night and you and your friend decide to go to the movies. You arrived early, so while you were seated waiting for the previews to come on, your friend turned to you and said that the Tuesday night discount was good for the economy because it allowed people to save. That said he, was good for the economy. You retorted that saving may be good or bad for the economy. Your friend was puzzled, not understanding how saving could ever be bad for the economy. The previews and advertisements came on the screen, followed by the feature presentation which was quite enjoyable.

At the end of the movie, your friend was eager to hear how you concluded that saving may be bad for the economy.

Task

Your task is to relieve your friend's eagerness by explaining how saving may be good or bad for the economy.

Scenario 49: A Parade of "Marginals". Play the Game

Games can be used effectively as learning devices. Suppose there is a game called *Parade of Marginals* designed to help students in introductory macroeconomics learn and remember the concept of *marginal*. The game involves writing down as many marginal concepts used in introductory macroeconomics as you can. The player with the most marginal concepts after the time allotted wins the game.

Task

Your task is to play the game. In addition to writing down as many marginal concepts as you can, you are required to define each concept written down. Go ahead and play the game.

Scenario 50: The More You Save, the Less You Save—A Real Paradox

On the basis of the principle that saving is good for individuals and families, the government of Parsimonia is using a great deal of resources encouraging its citizens to save more. Pamphlets have been published and distributed, programs on radio and TV stations have been aired, and meetings have been held throughout Parsimonia all extolling the virtues of saving by individuals and firms. The landscape was punctuated with posters and billboards, and savings plans have been established by which individuals receive tax benefits by saving. No stones have been left unturned in providing incentives to save. Saving was seen as the vehicle by which future prosperity was to be assured. The citizens of Parsimonia rose to the occasion and significantly increased their savings. It turned out that at some future date, the amount of savings in Parsimonia actually declined.

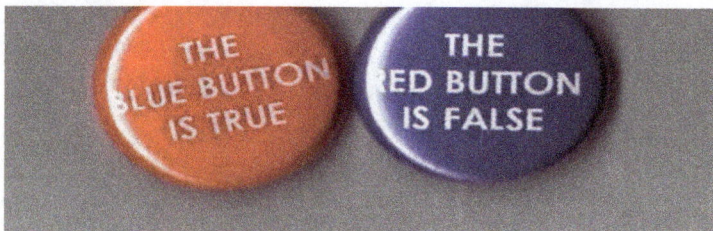

Task

Your task is to explain how an increase in saving can result in a reduction in saving.

Scenario 51: Funny (Not Phony) Math—The Multiplier

Your niece, an 11th-grade student, is very good at mathematics. You are at your desk studying the multiplier theory in economics.

The specific problem you are working on is this:

In a certain economy, it is given that the marginal propensity to consume (MPC) is 0.8 and the equilibrium level of income is $615 billion. What effect will an increase in investment of $15 billion have on the equilibrium level of income?

Your niece says, "Oh! That is so easy. All you have to do is to add the $15 billion to the $615 billion, and you have the answer, $630 billion. That MPC stuff is just put in there to through you off."

Task

Your task is to ignore your niece and solve the problem.

PART III

MONEY, BANKING, MONETARY THEORY & MONETARY POLICY

※

Scenario 52: A Moneyless Community Wherein Dwells No Inflation

You have most likely heard of a barter system where goods and services were traded without the use of money, and have probably wondered how such a system worked. A world traveller from your country had just returned from a far-off country. He spoke of visiting a large village where money did not exist. People gathered at the community center twice weekly to trade goods and services. He noted that it often took a long time for a transaction to be made because each trader, trader A, for example, had to find a trader, trader B, for example, who had what A wanted and who wanted what A was trading. He said that he spoke with some of the residents and none of them had ever heard of inflation.

Task

You are to explain why there can be no inflation in a barter economy.

Scenario 53: Notes on Desirable Characteristics of Money—The Textbook Cannot Tell All

Upon graduation from the Best School of Economics (BSE)—a fictitious university, you got employment as an economics instructor at Big Deal College (BDC)—also a fictitious college. One of the courses assigned to you was Principles of Macroeconomics. Upon reviewing the prescribed textbook, you observed that it was lacking in certain details. Specifically, you found that it did not mention the characteristics of money and you thought that was an important omission.

Task

Your task is to prepare notes (hand-outs) of about 400 words for your class on *Desirable Characteristics of Money*.

Scenario 54: Money and Monetary Policy Basics Via Pamphlets

MONEY

BOOK

Assume that you have recently graduated from university with a degree in economics, with a specialization in monetary economics. You have landed a job with New Economic Research Foundation (NERF), a hypothetical economic research institute that prepares short economic brochures and pamphlets on various aspects of economics for distribution to the public. Your job as an Economic Consultant is to assist the Chief Economic Consultant in preparing these pamphlets which are intended to serve as good sources of economic education. In particular, the Chief Economic Consultant has assigned to you the following duties:

a) Prepare Pamphlet A, describing the economic functions of money in a modern society. (300 words)

b) Prepare Pamphlet B, explaining how monetary policy can be used to control inflation in a modern money economy. Use the money market model, the rate of interest/investment relationship, and the AD/AS model. (300 words)

c) Prepare Pamphlet C, explaining the reasons for holding money, according to John Maynard Keynes. (300 words)

Your document will be in the form of three booklets with a total of approximately 900 words.

The Board of Directors of the Lending Bank of Commerce (a fictitious bank) meets once a month to discuss the direction of the bank. After the preliminaries and reports were given, one board member commented on the

significant progress that the LDC (Lending Bank of Commerce) has made over the past two years. She emphasized that in addition to earning good profits, LDC was creating money and adding to the quantity of money by lending out its excess reserves. She concluded by saying that the more the bank could do this (i.e., lend out its excess reserves), the brighter the bank's future would be.

Task

The board member has made a critical error in her comment. Your task is to identify the error and correct it.

Scenario 56: Monetary Policy to Combat Inflation and Recession—A Two-edged Sword?

Suppose that you are an employee at the central bank in the role of an economics clerk. You are employed in the policy section of the bank, and your main function is to use macroeconomic models to explain and solve current macroeconomic problems and issues. The latest statistics reveal that the economy has begun to show signs of inflationary pressures. While your immediate supervisor is occupied with preparations for a policy meeting with the Governor of the bank, he/she has asked you to prepare a document to be used in his/her meeting with the Governor of the bank.

Task

Specifically, you are to come up with a model that explains how monetary policy can be used to combat the looming inflationary situation. In the long-term economic forecast, the economy is predicted to slow down significantly and may even head for a recession. Therefore, your supervisor has asked you, since you are dealing with a model, to illustrate how monetary policy might also be used to head off a recession. (Hint: Use the AD/AD model).

Present your report in an essay of about 350 words.

Scenario 57: Tell It with Graphs: Money Matters

In addition to your task above (Scenario 56), your supervisor has asked you to prepare a set of AD/AS diagrams (graphs) to show how each of the following events will affect the equilibrium real GDP and the equilibrium price level, other things being equal.

a) The central bank increases the money supply when the economy is operating in the Keynesian range of the AS curve.
b) The central bank reduces the money supply when the economy is operating in the classical range of the AS curve.
c) The central bank reduces interest rates when the economy is operating in the intermediate range of the AS curve.
d) The central bank conducts a tight (contractionary) monetary policy when the economy is operating in the Keynesian range of the AS curve.

Scenario 58: Presentation at the Money Convention

Each year, economists of all persuasions meet in different parts of the world for a money convention. This year, the meeting is scheduled to be held in New Orleans, and your boss, a neoclassical economist who is an expert on monetary theory, has accepted an invitation to deliver a paper on monetary theory. Below is an audience similar to the one that your boss will be addressing.

As her assistant, your boss has asked you to prepare a section of her presentation dealing with the quantity theory of money.

Task

Your task is to prepare a 600-word document on the quantity theory of money so that your boss can include it in her presentation.

Scenario 59: Quantitative Easing! Is this a New Concept or Is It Just a New Name for an Old Concept?

In recent times, the term quantitative easing has gained popularity. The Governor of the central bank was invited to your university to talk about quantitative easing. On the appointed day, the hall where he was speaking was filled to capacity with economics students, finance students, and professors who all wanted to hear the address by the Governor. He did not disappoint them. His presentation was simple, lucid, and passionate. It was obvious that he believed in the effectiveness of quantitative easing as an instrument of monetary policy.

During a brief question period, one student of monetary economics commented that quantitative easing sounded a lot like open market operations and wanted to know if there was a difference. The Governor thanked her for the question and proceeded to explain the difference.

Task

Since you were one of the students who heard and thoroughly understood the Governor's talk, you are required to explain the idea of quantitative easing and how it is different from open-market operations.

Scenario 60: Newspaper Reports Policy Makers' Talk. Fiscal Policy vs Monetary Policy

On one of your daily commutes to work by train, you observed a newspaper on the vacant seat beside you. One of the headlines read: *Policy Makers Talk*. Unable to resist the temptation to read the article, you picked up the paper. You discovered that the talk was between the Minister of Finance and the Governor of the central bank. They spoke of economic policy variables. The Finance Minister spoke more of fiscal policy variables while the Governor of the Central Bank spoke more about monetary policy variables. By the time you finished reading the article, the train had reached to your stop.

Task

You are required to distinguish between fiscal policy variables and monetary policy variables and explain their effects on GDP, employment, and inflation.

PART IV

OTHER MACROECONOMIC ISSUES

(Roger and William are having breakfast in the cafeteria when the following conversation ensues).

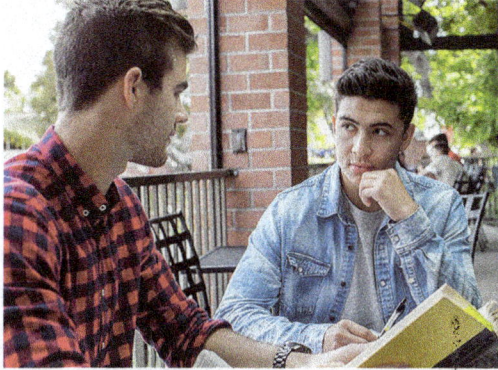

Roger: Did you know that the inflation that plagued the country in the 1970s was due to rapid increases in the price of oil?

William: Where did you get that information?

Roger: It's right here on the Internet.

William: Really? Let's see.

Roger: Here it is.

(They read)

"In 1973, the Organization of Petroleum Exporting Countries (OPEC) increased the price of oil by 70%. After that massive hike in the price of oil, the rate of inflation rose dramatically. For the very first time in several years, we have seen double-digit inflation. It therefore does not take much to conclude that the inflation of the 1970s was due to the rapid increase in the price of oil."

Roger: It must be true. It's right there on the Internet.

William: I guess so.

Task

Your task is to use this scenario to show that just because something is on the Internet does not mean that it's true.

Scenario 62: Stagflation. Oops! How Can This Be? Look to the Other Side

(Classroom setting with Professor Query, Eugene, Cathy, and other students)

Professor: Well then, according to Keynesian theory, if aggregate expenditure is less than aggregate output, firms will reduce their production levels and lay off workers. What then is the cause of unemployment?

Cathy: Not enough spending, obviously.

Professor: That is correct. According to this view, unemployment is the result of a deficiency in aggregate expenditure. Let's look at inflation now. If aggregate expenditure persistently exceeds potential output, then inflation will result. What then is the cause of inflation?

Eugene: Too much spending.

Professor: That's right. So unemployment is the result of not enough spending and inflation is the result of too much spending. We cannot have not enough spending and too much spending at the same time.

Student: It's only logical.

Professor: This brings us to stagflation—the simultaneous existence of high rates of unemployment and high rates of inflation.

Student: Stagflation cannot occur because we cannot have a deficiency in spending and excess spending at the same time.

Professor: History records that stagflation is real. The economy has experienced stagflation. Your assignment, class, is to explain how it is possible for stagflation to occur in an economy.

Task

Your task is to do Professor Query's assignment.

Scenario 63: Return to DeFicitia—A Matter of Stagflation

You may recall that DeFicitia is a fictitious country with a deficit problem. Now, the problem that faces DeFicitia is a high rate of inflation accompanied by a high rate of unemployment—a problem referred to as stagflation. Incomes policies (wage and price controls) have been suggested to the Government of DeFicitia to solve the problem of stagflation, but there is no political will to implement incomes policies in DeFicitia.

Unemployment 15%

Inflation 14%

Task

Your task is to suggest a solution to DeFicitia's problem of stagflation that does not include incomes policies.

Scenario 64: What Kind of Trap You Say? When Monetary Policy Fails.

No! No!

In a certain economy, interest rates have fallen to historically low levels. A Keynesian economist at the central bank is concerned that at such low levels of interest rates, monetary policy might not be effective in stimulating the economy which is showing signs of slowing down to the extent that a recession is likely if appropriate pre-emptive measures are not taken. She has suggested to the Governor of the bank to advise the Minister of Finance to use fiscal policy to rectify the situation.

Task

Your task is to explain the situation of the economy as described by the economist and to show that in that situation, expansionary monetary is unlikely to be effective.

Scenario 65: A Class Project—Rational Expectations

In your macroeconomics class, each student is required to write a short paper on one aspect of macroeconomics. Different topics such as causes of inflation, types of unemployment, supply-side policies, the life-cycle hypothesis, monetary policy tools, fiscal policy tools, problems with a huge public debt, theories of the business cycle, etc. were written on pieces of paper and placed in a box from which each student drew a topic without being able to see inside the box. When it was your turn, you drew the rational expectations hypothesis.

Task

Your task is to write a short paper (about 470 words) on the Rational Expectation Hypothesis.

You have been studying for a while so you decided to take a break. You turned on the TV and used the remote control to see if you could find anything interesting. Flipping through the channels, you noticed a panel discussion on taxes.

Although you were looking for something more relaxing, you paused to hear and see what the participants were saying. One member of the panel asked another member whether or not inflation was a tax. The member questioned responded that inflation was indeed a tax but declined to explain for lack of time. Your interest was aroused because you had never heard of an inflation tax. You decided to research the topic.

Task

Your task is to write a short document on inflation tax.

PART V

BALANCE OF PAYMENTS AND EXCHANGE RATES

Scenario 67: Currency Tied to Oil?

Oilando (an imaginary country) is well endowed with huge oil reserves scattered all over the country. Undercan (another imaginary country) is a close neighbour of Oilando. Both countries have very close economic ties. Undercan buys the vast majority of Oilando's oil exports, and most of Oilando's imports come from Undercan. Oilando has a flexible exchange rate system.

The demand for oil is known to be highly inelastic which means that a change in the price of oil has negligible effect on the quantity demanded. It has been observed over the years that whenever the price of oil rises, the value of the Oilando dollar in terms of the Undercan dollar rises as well. This is true for more than 90% of the time.

Task

Your task in this scenario is to explain why the value of the Oilando dollar rises in terms of the Undercan dollar when the price of oil rises.

Scenario 68: A Pamphlet on the Central Bank and Foreign Exchange

It has been four months since you prepared three pamphlets for New Economic Research Foundation (NERF). See Scenario 54. Being completely satisfied with your work on those pamphlets, the Chief Economic Consultant has assigned you the task of preparing another pamphlet.

Task

Your task is to prepare a pamphlet (about 300 words) explaining how the central bank intervenes in the foreign exchange market to maintain a fixed exchange rate.

Scenario 69: How Much Does It Cost? Can I Afford It? It's British. That Depends on the Exchange Rate

A Canadian by the name of David spent a year in England and fell in love with the Land Rover, a British car. On his return to Canada, he decided to purchase a Land Rover. He learned from a Canadian Land Rover dealer that the car he wanted would cost £35,000. The maximum amount of money that David was willing to spend on the car was $65,000 CAD. The exchange rate between the British £ and the CAD$ was £1 = CAD $1.95.

Task

Your task is to determine:

1. If David can afford to buy the car
2. What the exchange rate would have to be to enable him to afford the car.

Scenario 70: To Flex or Not to Flex: Advantages and Disadvantages of Flexible Exchange Rates

Your study group (see Scenario 36) has been doing really well. It demonstrates that "iron sharpens iron". The advantages of the *division of labour* are exemplified in your study group. You are now studying exchange rates and in the usual lottery, you drew the *advantages and disadvantages of flexible exchange rates*.

Task

Your task is to prepare notes on the *Advantages and Disadvantages of Flexible Exchange Rates* to be distributed to your study group.

Scenario 71: To Peg or Not to Peg: Advantages and Disadvantages of Fixed Exchange Rates

Based on the excellent job you did in preparing notes on the business cycle and on the advantages and disadvantages of flexible exchange rates (see Scenarios 36 and 70 above), you have been assigned the task of preparing notes for the group on the advantages and disadvantages of fixed exchange rates.

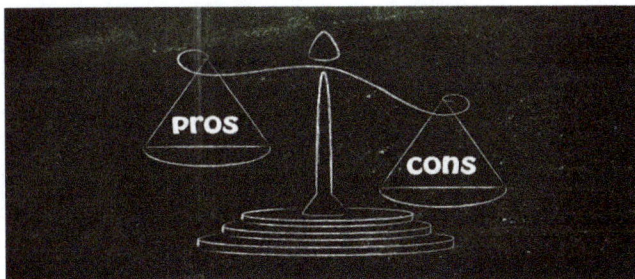

Task

You are to prepare notes on the Advantages and Disadvantages of Fixed Exchange Rates to be distributed to your study group.

PART VI

SOMEWHAT INTEGRATIVE

Scenario 72: Monetary Policy to Stimulate Economic Activity. Putting It Together

Toward the end of the school semester, a professor of macroeconomics wants to ensure that her students can combine different but related theories to explain how a particular economic policy would work to solve a particular economic problem. The following assignment was therefore assigned: How can the following theories be combined into an explanation of how monetary policy can be used to stimulate an economy that is suffering from a recession?

♦ The theory of interest rate determination (money market)
♦ The theory of the relationship between the rate of interest and the level of investment
♦ The theory of the relationship between spending and output and employment (AD/AS model)

Use graphs to illustrate each theory.

Task

Your task is to do the assignment.

Scenario 73: A Matter of Crowding Out. Why An Increase in Government Spending Might Not Be Expansionary.

On Thursday evenings, while their wives are out doing the grocery shopping, Dan, Paul, and Jim (Scenario 6) play dominos at one of their homes. On this particular Thursday evening, it was Jim's turn to host the gang. Since they are economists, they cannot resist "talking shop" while they play.

Jim: Hey Dan! Are you still teaching that an increase in government spending is expansionary?

Dan: Well, of course. Government spending is expansionary. That is why we call it "expansionary" fiscal policy.

Paul: Are you two at it again? Let's just play.

Dan: Well, Jim always seems to be attacking conventional wisdom. Everyone except him knows that when government spending increases, income will rise, and when income rises, consumers and firms spend more. This results in an increase in total spending, and any policy that results in an increase in aggregate expenditure is expansionary.

Jim: Well, in Governia (a fictitious country) government has been increasing it's spending in order to stimulate the economy but aggregate expenditure has not increased and the economy remains unstimulated. What do you have to say to that?

Dan: That's just an isolate case. There could be other factors.

Paul: Jim, can you pass me the chips, please? And let's play dominos.

Jim and Dan: Good idea!

Task

Your task is to explain Jim's assertion that an increase in government spending may not be expansionary.

Scenario 74: A Peek at General Equilibrium Analysis: Raising the Bar

You are teaching an introductory course called Principles of Macroeconomics. You are using an excellent textbook with lots of supplementary material. You believe, however, that your students should be introduced to general equilibrium analysis as it will lay a good foundation for further studies in economics should the students decide to continue their studies in economics. The problem, however, is that although there is an ample supply of material on general equilibrium analysis at a more advanced level, there is hardly anything suitable for your course. You remind them of the market interaction shown in the circular flow model, but you now want to raise the bar.

Task

Your task is to prepare for your students a suitable hand-out on general equilibrium analysis that will fill the gap.

Scenario 75: Can You Spot Them in There? Demand and Supply in the Circular Flow Model

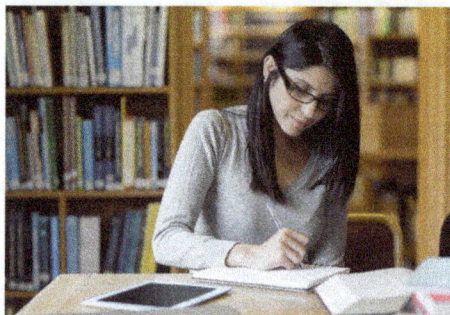

You have spent a generous amount of time studying the circular flow model. You know it well. You have explained it to your best friend (see Scenario 14) but you have never considered any notion of demand and supply in it. Of course, common sense dictates that if there are markets, there must be demand and supply, but you have never given it any serious thought. Now, it is almost at the end of the semester and your economics professor has given this final assignment:

"Examine the circular flow model and indicate all cases of demand and supply in the model."

Task

Your task is to do the assignment.

PART VII

SAMPLE TESTS

Answer All Questions   Time Allowed: I hour & 15 min.

PART 1: DEFINITIONS (10 MARKS)

1. Define each of the following terms. (Give an example if possible)

(a) Social science

(b) Positive statement

(c) Rent

(d) Production possibility (p-p) schedule

(e) Product market

PART 2: MULTIPLE-CHOICE (20 MARKS)

Select the letter that corresponds with the correct answer.

2. Which of the following is true about the study of economics?

a. It is is guaranteed to make you rich

b. It helps you to think logically

c. It guarantees that you will always be able to find a job

d. You will have a perfect understanding of how the economy of any country works.

3. Economists work in:

a. private firms such as banks and large manufacturing companies

b. colleges and universities

c. international organizations such as the World Bank

d. all of the above

4. Which of the following is scarce (in a relative sense) even in a land flowing with milk and honey? (Jorobel?)

a. Natural resources such as rivers and lakes

b. Human resources

c. Capital such as roads and equipment

d. All of the above

5. Profit is the income earned from:

a. financial capital

b. entrepreneurial services

c. real capital

d. land

6. The scientific method or approach involves:

a. observation and measurement

b. verification through testing

c. the formulation of hypotheses

d. all of the above

7. An economic model is:

a. just like a real economy in all respects

b. a simplified version of a real economy

c. always very easy to understand

d. none of the above

8. A hypothesis is:

a. a statement that is known to be true
b. the same as a normative statement
c. a statement that can be verified by testing
d. always stated in mathematical terms

9. Which of the following is true of positive statements?

a. They refer to facts

b. They deal with what is, was, or will be

c. They can be verified

d. All of the above

10. The main difference between positive statements and normative statements is that:

a. positive statements are always true while normative statements may be true or false

b. positive statements can be verified while normative statements cannot be verified

c. positive statements are based on emotions while normative statements are based on facts

d. positive statements are a part of economic study while normative statements are not.

11. Which of the following is true?

a. A stock is a constant while a flow is a variable

b. A flow is a constant while a stock is a variable

c. Neither stocks nor flows are variables

d. Stocks and flows are both variables

12. Economists use:

a. only endogenous variables

b. only exogenous variables

c. both endogenous and exogenous variables

d. neither endogenous nor exogenous variables

13. The opportunity cost of an item is:

a. the amount of money it costs to produce the item

b. the amount of money for which the item is sold

c. the best alternative given up in order to get the item

d. all of the above

14. A production possibility diagram shows all of the following except:

a. scarcity

b. choice

c. price

d. opportunity cost

15. If an economy is operating under conditions of increasing opportunity cost, its production possibility (p-p) curve will be:

a. concave and upward sloping

b. concave and downward sloping

c. linear and upward-sloping

d. linear and downward-sloping

16. Which of the following will cause a country's p-p curve to shift to the right?

a. It acquires better technology

b. It produces a greater quantity of goods and services

c. It uses unemployed resources

d. All of the above

17. Indicate whether the following statement is true or false.

A point that lies above a p-p curve is neither desirable nor attainable.
a True
b. False

18. If an economy decides to produce more goods and services by using unemployed resources, the opportunity cost of the additional goods and services is:

a. the payment made for the resources that it uses to produce the additional goods and services

b. the cost of producing the additional goods and services

c. nothing

d. the revenue or income received from selling the additional goods and services

19. Which of the following is not a macroeconomic issue?

a. The level of aggregate production of goods and services in an economy

b. The prices that a firm charges for its products

c. The level of employment in a country

d. The variation of total production in an economy from time to time.

20. Consider the simple circular flow model. In the factor market:

a. the buyers are the firms while the sellers are the households

b. the buyers are the households while the sellers are the firms

c. firms are both buyers and sellers

d. households are both buyers and sellers.

21. In the circular flow model:

a. real flows are money flows

b. real flows are payments for the resources

c. real flows are flows of goods and services and flows of resources

d. there are no money flows.

PART 3: PROBLEMS AND EXERCISES (5 MARKS)

22. Use production possibility diagrams (graphs) to show how each of the following will affect an economy's production possibility curve. Assume that the economy produces furniture (F) and smartphones (S), and that it operates under conditions of **increasing opportunity cost.** Put smartphones on the vertical axis and furniture on the horizontal axis.

(a) A fall in the prices of furniture and an increase in the prices of smartphones

(b) An increase in technology that positively affects the production of smartphones but not furniture

(c) Workers in the furniture industry are laid off because of a fall in demand for furniture.

(d) Workers are imported into the country to work in the smartphone industry.

(e) The government increases the taxes on the sale of both smartphones and furniture.

PART 4: ESSAY QUESTION (5 MARKS)

23. (a) What is an economic model?

(b) Why do economists construct and use models?

Answer All Questions   Time Allowed: 1 Hour & 15 min.

PART 1: DEFINITIONS (10 MARKS)

1. Define each of the following terms, giving examples, if possible.

(a) Real capital
(b) Flow
(c) Relative scarcity
(d) Endogenous variable
(e) Positive statement

PART 2: MULTIPLE CHOICE (20 MARKS)

Select the letter that corresponds with the correct answer.

2. Scarcity could be eliminated as an economic problem if:

a. people would learn to cooperate instead of compete

b. sufficient new reserves of natural resources were discovered

c. output per hour of human labour were increased one hundredfold

d. none of the above

3. Which aspect of human behavior <u>most</u> concerns the economist?

a. The voting pattern in a society and state government

b. The behavior of people as members of a group or organization

c. The behavior of individuals and groups engaged in the process of production, distribution, and consumption

c. Public attitude towards social issues

4. Economists assume that:

a. resources are unlimited but wants are limited
b. resources are limited but wants are unlimited
c. both resources and wants are unlimited
d. both resources and wants are limited

5. Economics is not a science because:

a. human behaviour cannot be studied scientifically

b. mathematics cannot be used effectively in economics

c. economists cannot conduct controlled experiments

d. none of the above

6. A good economic model is one that:

a. contains as many variables as possible

b. is dependent on sophisticated mathematics

c. successfully and consistently explains or predicts economic events

d. does not need assumptions

7. Choice is a direct result of:

a. ambition

b. scarcity

c. extravagance

d. none of the above.

8. Economists construct models in order to:

a. impress non-economists

b. restrict entry into the economics profession

c. make it easier to understand how a real economy works

d. introduce as many variables as possible into their analysis.

9. Disagreement among economists is due to:

a. the fact that economics is not a science

b. the fact that economic models are often expressed verbally instead of mathematically

c. the fact that some economists just don't understand the complexities of modern mathematics used in economic models

d. the fact that economists have different values, or they may use different economic models to explain the same economic phenomenon.

10. Which of the following is a flow?

a. The number of graduates entering the labour force each year

b. The number of students in the cafeteria at 2:00 p.m. on February 23

c. The amount of money in your purse or wallet

d. All of the above are flow variables

11. If two variables move together in the same direction, they are said to be:

a. endogenous variables

b. directly related

c. exogenous variables

d. inversely related

12. Microeconomics deals with:

a. small and unimportant economic issues only

b. only small economic sectors where only few people are employed

c. the behaviour of individual economic units

d. all of the above

13. Factors of production are:
a. scarce in advanced countries but abundant in poor countries
b. required to produce goods but not services
c. scarce in poor countries but abundant in rich countries
d. scarce in both rich and poor countries

14. Economists classify resources into the following categories:

a. Available, scarce, expensive, and natural

b. Land, labour, capital, and entrepreneurship

c. Artificial, financial, human, and manufactured

d. Natural, imported, limitless, and personal

15. The reward for capital is called:

a. rent

b. interest/dividend

c. wages

d. profit

16. The opportunity cost of an item is:

a. the market price of the item expressed in money

b. the monetary cost of the resources used to produce the item

c. the profit obtained from the sale of the item

d. None of the above

17. A production possibility curve shows:

a. the boundary between combinations of goods/services that are attainable through production and those that are unattainable

b. all combinations of goods/services consumed by the economy

c. the total value of all goods/services produced by the economy

d. all possible ways of producing the economy's output of goods/services

18. A linear (straight line) p-p curve, with corn and books on the axes, implies that:

a. the monetary cost of producing corn equals the monetary cost of producing books

b. the economy can only produce equal quantities of corn and books

c. books and corn are perfect substitutes

d. none of the above

19. A production possibility curve showing increasing opportunity cost is:

a. linear and upward sloping

b. convex and downward sloping

c. linear and downward sloping

d. concave and downward sloping

20. Which of the following will cause a country's p-p curve to shift to the right?

a. The country acquires more resources
b. The country increases production by hiring previously unemployed workers
c. Prices in the country fall
d. All of the above

21. A situation in which the economy cannot produce more of one commodity without producing less of some other commodity is called:

a. production inability
b. a state of unattainability
c. productive inefficiency
d. productive efficiency

PART 3: PROBLEMS AND EXERCISES (5 MARKS)

22. Use production possibility diagrams (graphs) to show how each of the following will affect an economy's production possibility curve. Assume that the economy produces computers (C) and bread (B), and that it operates under conditions of **increasing opportunity cost**. Put computers on the vertical axis and bread on the horizontal axis.

(a) The country switches some resources from computer production to bread production.

(b) The country discovers resources that can be used **only** in bread production.

(c) Unemployed workers leave the country.

(d) Firms use previously unemployed resources to increase their production of computers and bread.

(e) The economy decides to abandon its production of computers and bread.

PART 4: ESSAY QUESTION (5 MARKS)

23. (a) What is an economic model? (1 mark)

(b) Why do economists construct models? (2 marks)

(c) How can one determine the "goodness" of a model? (2 marks)

Answer All Questions   Time Allowed: 1 hour & 15 min.

PART 1. DEFINITIONS (10 MARKS)

1. Define each of the following terms, giving examples, if possible.

a. Supply curve

b. Equilibrium price

c. Normal good

d. Intermediate product (in national income accounting)

Net domestic income at factor cost (NDI)

PART 2. MULTIPLE-CHOICE (20 MARKS)

Select the letter that corresponds with the correct answer.

2. A market can exist without:

a. a physical place

b. A price

c. sellers

d. buyers

3. If the supply curve for pens is upward sloping, then an increase in the price of pens will result in a(n):

a. increase in the supply of pens

b. decrease in the supply of pens

c. increase in the quantity of pens supplied

d. decrease in the quantity of pens supplied.

4. Consider hotdogs and ketchup to be complements. If the price of hotdogs rises, we would expect:

a. an increase in the demand for ketchup

b. a decrease in the demand for ketchup

c. a decrease in the demand for hotdogs

d. both b and c.

5. A downward-sloping demand curve for an item shows that:

a. buyers will be willing and able to buy less as the price falls

b. buyers will be willing and able to buy more as the price falls

c. sellers will be willing and able to sell more as the price rises

d. sellers will not be affected by a change in price.

6. If a surplus exists at a specific price, then it means that:

a. sellers want to sell a greater quantity than what buyers want to buy

b. the market is not working well

c. the price is too high as far as sellers are concerned

d. buyers want to buy more than what sellers want to sell

7. If the demand for tablets (electronic) increases, other things being equal, then:

a. the equilibrium price of tablets will rise and the equilibrium quantity of tablets will also increase

b. the equilibrium price of tablets will fall, but the equilibrium quantity will rise

c. the equilibrium price and equilibrium quantity of tablets both decrease

d. the equilibrium price of tablets will fall but the effect on equilibrium quantity is unknown.

8. Which of the following is likely to cause a decrease in demand for an item?

a. An increase in the price of the item

b. A decrease in the price of the item

c. A decrease in the number of buyers

d. A fall in the number of sellers

9. Which of the following is likely to cause the supply curve for a product to shift to the left?

a. A decrease in the price of the product
b. An increase in the cost of producing the product
c. A fall in demand
d. All of the above

10. In the simple circular flow model, resources flow from households to the:

a. product market
b. factor market
c. financial market
d. none of the above

11. Household sell resources for:

a. wages, rent, interest & dividends, and profits

b. wages only

c. consumption, investment, and imports

d. capital consumption (Depreciation)

12. In the product market:

a. the buyers are firms and the sellers are households

b. the sellers are firms and the buyers are households

c. the buyers and sellers are households

d. the buyers and sellers are firms

13. In the simple circular flow model:

a. firms buy resources in the factor market and sell them in the product market

b. firms buy goods and services in the resource market and sell resources in the product market

c. firms buy resources in the factor market and sell products in the goods and services market

d. households sell goods and services in the factor market and buy resources in the product market

14. GDP measures:

a. the value of all goods and serves sold in an economy

b. the market value of all goods and services imported into the country

c. the market value of all the resources used to produce the economy's output of goods and services during a period of time

d. the market value of all final goods and services produced in an economy during a period of time

15. Two methods of measuring the GDP are:

a. the double-counting method and depreciation methods

b. the circular flow and factor income methods

c. the income and expenditure methods

d. the demand and supply methods

16. Capital consumption allowance (depreciation) is:

a. a statement of capital accumulation

b. the value of the capital stock

c. the loss of value of the capital stock through use or time

d. subtracted from net national income to obtain gross national income.

17. If C= consumption, W = wages and salaries, D = depreciation, I = investment, X = exports, i = interest and dividends, G = government spending, M = imports, T_{IB} = indirect business taxes, R = rent, π = profits, then GDP_Y (income-based) can be calculated by the following formula:

a. $GDP_Y = C + I + G + (X - M)$

b. $GDP_Y = W + R + C + i + G$

c. $GDP_Y = W + R + I + \pi + T_{IB} + D$

d. $GDP_Y = W + R + i + \pi + D + T_{IB}$

18. If net investment (I_N) = $1,000, and depreciation (D) is $200, gross investment (Ig) will be:

a. $500

b. $800

c. $1,200

d. $2,000

19. Which of the following is an example of an intermediate product?

a. Lumber

b. A laptop computer

c. A pen

d. A chair in a classroom

20. Which of the following would <u>not</u> be included in GDP?

a. A government grant to a student

b. The wages paid to a gardener

c. The work performed by a housekeeper

d. Flowers sold by a florist.

21. The purchase of an airline ticket by a family would be accounted for in:

a. GDP income-based

b. GDP expenditure-based

c. intermediate products

d. both a and b.

PART 3. PROBLEMS AND EXERCISES (5 MARKS)

22. Use demand and supply diagrams (graphs) to show the effect of each of the following events on the equilibrium price and equilibrium quantity of reading lamps. (**Consider reading lamps as normal goods and assume that other things remain equal**).

Enrolment in colleges and universities decreases drastically

An announcement by reputable scientists that reading lamps preserve vision

A decrease in the cost of producing reading lamps

The discovery of a more efficient method of producing reading lamps

An overall increase in consumers' income.

PART 4. ESSAY QUESTION (5 MARKS)

23. Why is GDP not a good measure of societal well-being? (Three points will suffice).

Answer All Questions   Time Allowed: 1 hour & 15 min.

PART 1. DEFINITIONS

1. Define each of the following terms, giving examples, if possible.

a. Demand schedule

b. Equilibrium quantity

c. Inferior good

d. Double counting (in national income accounting)

e. The underground economy

PART 2. MULTIPLE-CHOICE (20 MARKS)

Select the letter that corresponds with the correct answer.

2. The market process refers to:

a. the methods used by merchants to take their products to market

b. the various rules and regulations governing behavior in markets

c. the means by which a government sets the price of an item in the market

d. the process by which buyers and sellers exchange goods and services.

3. In a demand schedule, a price of $6.00 is associated with a quantity of 100 units. This tells us that:

a. the demand is 600 units

b. the demand is $6.00

c. the item will be sold for $6.00 per unit

d. none of the above.

4. Tide and Breeze are substitutes as detergents. If the price of Breeze rises, other things being equal:

a. the quantity of Breeze demanded will fall

b. the demand for Breeze will not be affected

c. the demand for Tide will increase

d. all of the above.

5. A downward-sloping demand curve for an item implies that:

a. demand will increase as price falls

b. a greater quantity will be demanded as price falls

c. price and quantity demanded are positively (directly) related

d. a smaller quantity will be bought at any price.

6. If a shortage exists at a specific price, then it means that:

a. sellers want to sell a greater quantity than what buyers want to buy

b. the market is not working well

c. the price is too high as far as sellers are concerned

d. buyers want to buy more than what sellers want to sell

7. If the demand increases, other things being equal, we predict:

a. an increase in price and a decrease in quantity

b. an increase in price and an increase in quantity

c. a decrease in price and an increase in quantity

d. a decrease in price and a decrease in quantity.

8. Which of the following is likely to affect the supply of a product?

a. The cost of resources used to produce the product

b. A change in the technology used to produce the product

c. Weather conditions

d. All of the above.

9. Which of the following is likely to cause the supply curve for a product to shift to the right?

a. An increase in the price of the product

c. An increase in the demand for the product

b. A decrease in the cost of producing the product

d. All of the above

10. The flow of resources, goods and services, expenditures, and income between households and firms through markets is called:

a. the circular flow

b. the producers' circle

c. consumer sovereignty

d. none of the above.

11. Which of the following is a true statement?

a. The product market is the market in which firms sell resources

b. The factor market is the market in which firms buy finished goods and services

c. The product market is the market in which households buy resources

d. The factor market is the market in which firms buy resources

12. Which of the following is correct?

a. Households and firms interact in the product and factor markets

b. Households and firms interact only in the factor market

c. Households and firms interact only in the product market

d. None of the above.

13. In the factor market:

a. the buyers are firms and the sellers are households

b. the sellers are firms and the buyers are households

c. the buyers and sellers are households

d. the buyers and sellers are firms

14. In the simple circular flow model, the flow of income from the factor market to households:

a. consists of wages, rent, interest and dividends, and profit

b. represents payment for factors of production

c. is a money flow as opposed to a real flow

d. all of the above

15. The total value of all goods and services produced within the borders of a country is that country's:

a. total investment in the country

b. gross domestic product (GDP)

c. total disposable income

d. none of the above

16. GDP income-based is calculated by adding:

a. all expenditures during the year

b. wages and other factor incomes, and subtracting indirect business taxes

c. exports and gross domestic spending

d. none of the above

17. Transfer payments include all of the following <u>except</u>:

a. government grants to students

b. social security payments

c. government financial assistance to farmers

d. government payment of civil servants.

18. If C= consumption, W = wages and salaries, D = depreciation, I = gross investment, X = exports, i = interest and dividends, G = government spending, M = imports, T_{IB} = indirect business taxes, R = rent, π = profits, then GDP$_E$ (expenditure-based) can be calculated by the following formula:

a. $GDP_E = C + W + G + (X - M)$

b. $GDP_E = W + R + C + I + G$

c. $GDP_E = W + R + i + \pi + T_{IB} + D$

d. $GDP_E = C + I + G + (X - M)$

19. If gross investment (I_G) = \$1,200, and depreciation (D) is \$200, Net investment (I_N) will be:

a. \$1,400

b. \$ 800

c. \$1,000

d. \$2,400

20. Which of the following is a non-marketed good or service?

a. Housework such as cooking and cleaning performed by a spouse

b. Volunteer work performed by college students

c. Garage chores performed as a hobby

d. All of the above

21. If P represents the price level, the formula for converting nominal GDP to real GDP is:

a. Real GDP = nominal GDP $\times$ P/100

b. Real GDP = nominal GDP $\times$ real GDP $\div$ 100P

c. Real GDP = nominal GDP $\times$ 100/P

d. None of the above.

PART 3. PROBLEMS AND EXERCISES (5 MARKS)

22. Use demand and supply diagrams (graphs) to show the effect of each of the following events on equilibrium price and equilibrium quantity of pencil cases. (**Consider pencil cases as normal goods and assume that other things remain equal).**

a. The government provides pens and pencils free of charge to elementary and high school students

b. An increase in the number of students going to school

c. An increase in the number of firms producing and selling pencil cases

d. An increase in the prices of material used to produce pencil cases

e. A significant decrease in the prices of pens and pencils.

PART 4. ESSAY QUESTION (5 MARKS)

23. What is the difference between GDP and GNP?

Test 3

PART 1. DEFINITIONS (10 MARKS)

1. Define each of the following terms

a. Fiscal policy

b. Balanced budget

c. Liquidity preference

d. Marginal efficiency of investment

e. Easy monetary policy

PART 2. MULTIPLE-CHOICE (20 MARKS)

2. Fiscal policy is conducted by:

a. local governments only

b. the federal government only

c. both the federal and local governments

d. the central bank

3. The idea of using fiscal policy to stimulate economic activity was first introduced by:

a. the classical economists

b. the monetarists

c. Keynes

d. none of the above

4. The main objectives of fiscal policy include:

a. full employment and high inflation

b. high employment and low inflation

c. economic stability

d. b and c

5. Which of the following statements is true?

a. The public debt is exactly the same as the deficit

b. The government can help to finance a deficit by raising taxes

c. The government borrows money from the public by selling bonds to the public

d. The government does not borrow from the central bank because it owns the bank.

6. A budget surplus means that:

a. there is too much money in the economy and the price level will rise

b. there is not enough money in the economy and the real GDP will fall

c. government spending is more than its tax revenues

d. government is spending less than it collects in taxes

7. Which of the following lends money to the federal government?

a. Ordinary citizens

b. Commercial banks

c. Residents of foreign countries

d. All of the above

8. If the economy is operating in the Keynesian range of the AS curve, then an expansionary fiscal policy that leaves the AD curve within the Keynesian range will:

a. increase real GDP and the price level

b. increase real GDP but leave the price level unchanged

c. increase the price level but leave real GDP unchanged

d. decrease real GDP and the price level

9. Which of the following will tend to have a contractionary effect on real GDP?

a. An increase in government spending

b. An increase in taxes

c. A reduction in income taxes

d. None of the above

10. Economists define money to include:

a. debit cards (interact)

b. major credit cards such as Visa and Master Card

c. cheques

d. none of the above

11. Which of the following is NOT money?

a. Central bank of notes (bills)

b. Coins

c. Debit cards

d. deposit money (demand deposits)

12. Money serves as a medium of exchange when:

a. we use it to pay for goods and services

b. it provides information about the value of an item

c. we store it for future use

d. all of the above

13. Money serves as a unit of account when:

a. we use it to pay for goods and services

b. it provides information about the value of an item

c. we store it for future use

d. none of the above

14. Barter exchange is inefficient because:

a. it is much too complicated

b. it requires a double-coincidence of wants

c. it focuses on only one side of the market

d. all of the above

15. Which of the following is the most liquid of *all* assets?

a. Government savings bonds

b. Debit cards

c. Money

d. None of them is liquid

16. According to Keynes, which of the following is a reason for holding money?

a. The transactions motive or demand

b. The precautionary motive or demand

c. The speculative motive or demand

d. All of the above

17. Which of the following exerts the greatest control over a country's money supply?

a. Commercial/chartered banks

b. The central bank

d. The government (Department of Finance)

d. The general public

18. The demand for money curve is:

a. upward sloping

b. vertical

c. downward sloping

d. horizontal

19. Any change in the money supply and interest rates is referred to as:

a. fiscal policy

b. monetary policy

c. stabilization policy

d. none of the above

20. Other things being equal, a decrease in the money supply will:

a. lower interest rates

b. shift the demand curve for money

c. raise interest rates

d. increase income

21. The appropriate monetary policy in an inflationary situation is:

a. a reduction in government spending (G) and an increase in taxes (T)

b. an increase in the money supply and a reduction in interest rates

c. a decrease in government spending and an increase in taxes

d. a decrease in the money supply and an increase in interest rates

PART 3. PROBLEMS AND EXERCISES (5 MARKS)

22. Use money market analysis (demand and supply for money graphs) to show the effect of each of the following events on the equilibrium rate of interest and the equilibrium quantity of money. Assume ceteris paribus. [You are to say what will happen to the equilibrium rate of interest (r) and the equilibrium quantity of money (M)].

a. A recession that reduces the level of income in the economy.

b. The monetary authorities increase the money supply.

c. The central bank conducts an expansionary monetary policy.

d. Workers get a 10% increase in wages and salaries.

e. Consumers' incomes and business profits increase.

PART 4. ESSAY (5 MARKS)

23. Imagine that you are an economic advisor to the government and the central bank. (Big job, eh?) You observe that the economy is experiencing a rate of inflation that is unacceptable. What advice would you give to the government and the central bank about actions that they can take to improve the situation? (The AD/AS model will be useful here).

Answer All Questions   Time Allowed: 1 Hour & 15 min.

PART 1. DEFINITIONS (10 MARKS)

1. Define each of the following terms:

a. Aggregate demand (AD) <u>curve</u>

b. Keynesian range of the aggregate supply (AS) curve

c. Budget surplus

d. Liquid asset

e. Monetary policy

PART 2. MULTIPLE-CHOICE (20 MARKS)

2. The AD/AS model is a:

a. macroeconomic model

b. demand-side only model

c. microeconomic model

d. supply-side only model

3. The AD curve is:

a. upward sloping

b. horizontal

c. downward sloping

d. vertical

4. Which of the following will shift the AD curve to the right?

a. A fall in the price level

b. A widespread flood

c. An increase in the price level

d. An increase in investment

5. If the economy is operating in the classical range of the AS curve, we know that:

a. it cannot increase output

b. it can increase its output without putting much upward pressure on the price level

c. economic policy (fiscal policy or monetary policy) will have little or no effect on the economy

d. inflation will never happen

6. Which of the following is an AS shifter?

a. A forest fire that destroys large areas of forests

b. A wave of technological improvements

c. A significant increase in population through immigration

d. All of the above

7. Fiscal policy is conducted by:

a. the government
b. the central bank
c. both a and b
d. neither a nor b.

8. A government can finance a deficit by:

a. borrowing from the public

b. borrowing from the central bank

c. neither a nor b

d. both a and b.

9. The public debt is:

a. the amount of money the public owes the government in taxes

b. the amount of money the government owes its creditors

c. the amount by which government spending exceeds its tax revenue

d. none of the above

10. Money is defined as:

a. a country's stock of gold

b. any item used for final payment

c. debit cards (interact)

d. any liquid asset

11. Which of the following is the most liquid of all assets?

a. Bonds

b. Savings accounts

c. Money

d. None of the above

12. Which of the following is money?

a. Coins such as quarters, nickels, and dimes

b. Bills (notes) issued by the monetary authority

c. A chequing account

d. All of the above

13. Credit and debit cards are <u>not</u> money because:

a. they are made of plastic

b. they are not a medium of exchange

c. they cannot be used to obtain goods

d. they are too popular

14. Which of the following is an economic function of money?

a. Medium of exchange

b. Unit of account

c. Store of value

d. All of the above

15. Which of the following represents money serving as a measure of value?

a. The monthly payment of rent

b. A balance of $1,200 in a savings account

c. The price tag of $27.95 on a school bag

d. Paying $27.95 for a school bag

16. Which of the following exerts the greatest control over a country's money supply?

a. The residents of the country

b. The central bank

d. The commercial banks

d. The International Monetary Fund (IMF)

17. According to Keynes, the demand for money curve (liquidity preference) is:

a. upward sloping

b. vertical

c. downward sloping

d. horizontal

18. A change in the money supply and interest rates by the monetary authority is referred to as:

a. fiscal policy

b. monetary policy

c. budgetary policy

d. none of the above

19. Other things being equal, a decrease in the money supply will:

a. lower interest rates

b. shift the liquidity preference curve

c. raise interest rates

d. increase income

20. If the rate of interest falls:

a. the demand for money curve will shift to the right

b. the demand for money curve will shift to the left

c. the quantity of money demanded will increase

d. the quantity of money supplied will also fall.

21. The appropriate monetary policy in a situation of unemployment is:

a. an increase in government spending (G) and a decrease in taxes (T)

b. an increase in the money supply and a reduction in interest rates

c. a decrease in government spending an increase in taxes

d. a decrease in the money supply and an increase in interest rates

PART 3. PROBLEMS AND EXERCISES (5 MARKS)

22. Use the AD/AS model to show the effect of each of the following events on the equilibrium price level and real GDP. Assume ceteris paribus, and that the economy is operating in the intermediate range of the AS curve.

(You are to say what will happen to the equilibrium price level and real GDP after the event has occurred).

a. The government reduces its spending.

b. A wave of new and more efficient technology hits the country.

c. The central bank conducts a tight monetary policy. (Remember to use the AD/AS model)

d. The prices of important inputs fall and thus reduce the costs of production.

e. Consumers become optimistic about their future economic conditions.

PART 4. ESSAY (5 MARKS)

23. Imagine that you are an economic advisor to the government. You observe that the economy is experiencing a rate of unemployment that is unacceptable. What advice would you give to the government about actions that it can take to improve the situation? (The AD/AS model will be useful here).

ANSWERS

Scenario 1: Hiring an Economist

Companies are increasingly recognizing the importance of economists to the success of their businesses; hence, they are hiring economists either as paid employees or as consultants. At LVC, an economist could perform a variety of functions that could help the company to achieve its objectives. Here are a few ways that having an economist on board could help.

Pricing

The prices that LVC charges for its products will determine the level of its profits. Economists study markets and can therefore help the company to price its products so that it earns maximum profits. It may be necessary for LVC to change its prices from time to time, depending on circumstances. Having an economist on staff would help the company to determine the effects of price changes on its profitability.

Estimating future demand

It is of vital importance for a company to be able to forecast demand for its products. Decisions made under conditions of certainty are likely to be superior to those made under uncertainty. Demand forecasting greatly reduces the amount of uncertainty in the decision-making process. Economists are experts in demand forecasting. The company will be able to properly plan its production levels, determine its requirement for raw materials, and eliminate waste.

Policy impact

Government policies affect the economic environment within which companies operate and may affect companies directly. An economist could carefully analyze the impact of public policy and provide LVC with the relevant information so that it can appropriately respond to such policies.

Scenario 2: What exactly do Economists do?

Job description for an economist

Duties and responsibilities

The economist:

1. Provides relevant data by conducting research on economic issues
2. Determines trends by analyzing and interpreting data
3. Contributes to good decision-making by advising executives
4. Reports research findings by preparing reports, tables, and graphs
5. Solves economic problems by using appropriate economic models
6. Predicts economic outcomes by using statistical and econometric models
7. Increases overall effectiveness by collaborating with specialists from other disciplines.

Job requirements and skills

The economist should have a minimum of a master's degree in economics. He or she should possess excellent communication (written and oral) skills. The ability to work as a team member is a necessity.

Scenario 3: Economic Growth—A Controversial Issue? Applying Economic Reasoning

The benefits of economic growth are undeniable and are hardly in dispute. The controversial issue is whether or not the pursuit of more economic growth is desirable. The economic way of thinking can be applied to this situation so that a valid conclusion can be reached. As noted in the scenario, there are benefits (enumerated by the supporters of more growth) and there are costs (enumerated by the detractors of more growth). Economists make decisions at the margin. In considering a course of action, they weigh the additional benefits against the additional costs. If the extra benefits outweigh the extra costs of pursuing the course of action, then the action should be taken. Otherwise, the course of action should not be taken. The relevant question here is whether or not more economic growth should be pursued.

The following diagram will help to illustrate the decision-making process.

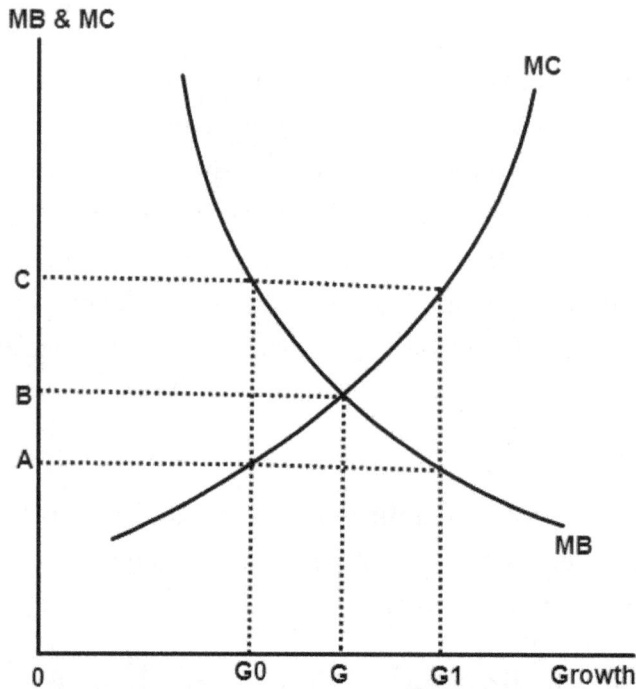

MB and MC are marginal benefits and marginal cost curves respectively. If the level of economic growth in Econoville is G0, then the additional benefit of pursuing further growth, C, exceeds the additional cost, A; therefore, additional growth should be pursued. On the other hand, if the level of growth is G1, the extra benefit of pursuing more growth, A, is less than the additional cost, C; therefore growth should be curtailed. At an economic growth of G, the marginal benefit is just equal to the marginal cost at B. This is the optimum amount of economic growth that Econoville should pursue.

Scenario 4: Economics, a Science? Never!

Dear Mr. Freeman,

I read your article about economics and I was appalled at your obvious ignorance of the subject. It is obvious that you have never studied economics, and if you did, then it has definitely escaped you. Let me enlighten you, Sir. In order to qualify as a science, a field of study must follow a certain procedure which is called the scientific approach. It involves data collection, observation, and measurement; the formulation of testable hypotheses; experimentation; and verification. This is the essence of science and this is how economists study the economy. So you see, Mr.

Freeman, economics does not claim to be a science; it *is* a science in every sense of the word.

Scenario 5: Why Don't They Listen? Economists as Advisers

Indeed, the recommendations of economic advisers are not always followed. Leaders often surround themselves with advisers in a variety of areas—political, communications, legal, etc. When the economic advisers report their recommendations, it is not that the Prime Minister and other leaders do not listen, but before they make a decision, they consider inputs from other advisers. It is not only the economic effects with which they are concerned. How will certain powerful interest groups react to the policy? Will the leader's support base be weakened by the policy? Will the policy be seen generally as the right thing to do? Leaders hear and weigh all these and other considerations before deciding what course of action to take. So for these reasons, although the economic advisers might do an excellent job in providing valuable input, their advice might not be followed.

Scenario 6: Economists at the Picnic. Disagreement among Economists

The issue between Dan and Paul on the tax matter is obviously normative in nature. They hold different opinions as to whether or not the tax should be imposed on cigarettes. Such differences in values and opinions are a major cause of disagreement among economists, and it is clearly reflected in the exchange between Dan and Paul. The issue regarding the extent to which a fall in the rate of interest affects the level of investment is a positive issue, yet Paul and Jim disagree. In this case, they disagree over the magnitude of the change. This type of disagreement may be prolonged because of the lack of adequate empirical data.

Scenario 7: A Land Flowing with Milk and Honey. Any Scarcity Here?

a) Miss Green and Mr. Brown seem to be looking at the vast array of resources and are puzzled by the notion of scarcity as applied to Jorobel. In an absolute sense, the country may be flowing with milk and honey. Abundance everywhere. The concept of scarcity that they must have had in mind is absolute scarcity.

b) Even in Jorobel, with its abundance of valuable resources, scarcity still exists. There would not be sufficient resources to enable Jorobel to produce all the goods and services that would be necessary to satisfy all the wants of all its citizens. Thus relative scarcity or economic scarcity exists even in Jorobel. Miss Green and Mr. Brown both face scarcity. In order to attend the party, they must sacrifice some other activity—maybe a quiet evening at home with their families.

c) **Scenario 8: The Cost of Attending University May Be More Than You Think**

d) An extremely important cost item that is missing from the calculation of John's total cost of attending university is the income that he could have earned instead of attending university. Economists refer to this type of cost as *opportunity cost.*

e) The total cost to John of attending university is all the cost items listed in the table plus the opportunity cost. That is $29,500 + $30,000 = $59,500.

f) If John was unemployed before he decided to attend university, then the opportunity of his attending university would be zero. Therefore his cost would be $29,500. One further consideration is the $6,500 that he pays for the room. This figure might have to be adjusted if John would live at home had he not decided to attend university.

Scenario 9: Enrolment Planning. Anything to do with Opportunity Cost?

At first glance, it would seem that the university administrator's view is correct. After all, attending university is costly—tuition fees, possible room and board, books, transportation, etc. are just some of the expenses involved. In a period of high unemployment, income tends to fall, so the ability to pay tuition fees tends to be less, resulting in a decrease in enrolment. However, when one considers the full cost of attending university, one must look not only at the direct expenses. The biggest cost is often the opportunity cost—the income the students could have earned instead of going to university. In deciding to attend university, one should consider the full cost of doing so. Other things being equal, the higher the cost of attending university, the lower the enrolment will be. During a period of high unemployment, the full cost of attending university is relatively low because the prospects of finding employment are low. The opportunity cost is practically zero so one should expect enrolment to increase. The consultant's view is correct, so those additional classrooms should be prepared.

Scenario 10: Calculating Real Profit. The Economist's Approach

The Income Statement provided for Bread of Life Bakery and Café shows that the bakery made a net profit of $290,500. Violet had good reason to smile when she looked at the bottom line. If she had accepted the position of manager of the competing bakery, she would have earned only $60,000 as salary which is significantly less than her earning from her bakery. But the figures in the Income Statement don't tell the whole story.

The Income Statement presented for Bread of Life has omitted a major cost item— the salary of $60,000 that Violet could have earned as manager of the competing bakery. Economists refer to this type of cost as *opportunity cost*. Adding this cost to the $309,500 recorded as operating expenses brings the true cost of operating the business to $369,500. So in reality then, it turns out that Violet's earnings, from an economic perspective, is $600,000 − 369,500 = $230,500. She has earned (230,500 − 60,000 = $170,000 more than she would have earned as manager of the competing bakery.

Scenario 11: Presentation for the Park. Explain It with Production Possibilities Curves

Series of Graphs for the Director of Parks and Recreation

The following series of production-possibility graphs will suffice.

a) The following graph shows that with its given budget, the Department of Parks and Recreation can provide many combinations of parking spaces and playground equipment. If the department is operating at point A, it can get more playground equipment by moving to point B, but that would entail giving up some parking spaces.

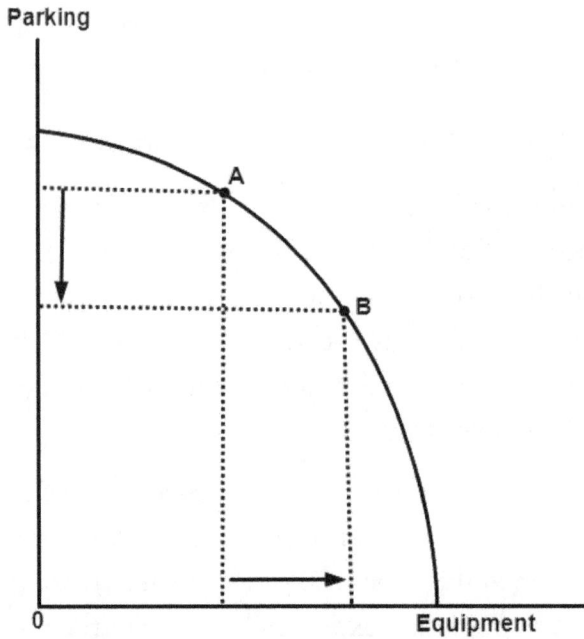

b) The production-possibility curve (PPC) will shift out as shown below. The ability to increase parking spaces will rise while the ability to provide more playground equipment will be unaffected. The shift in the PPC is non-parallel.

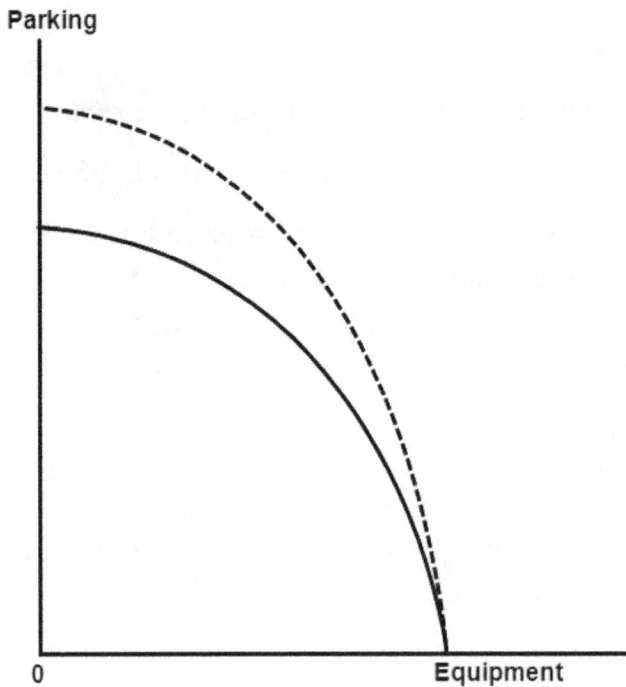

c) The increase in demand for parking spaces will have no effect on the Department's ability to provide parking spaces or playground equipment; hence the department's PPC will not be affected. As shown in the diagram below, the curve does not shift.

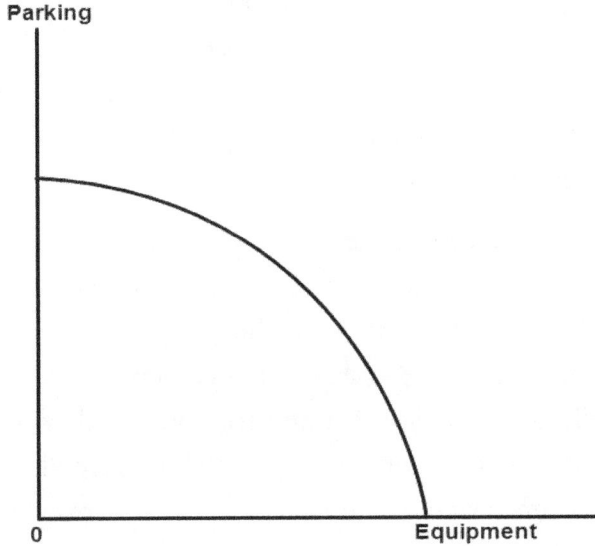

d) An increase in the budget for the Department of Parks and Recreation means that the department will be able to provide both more playground equipment *and* more parking spaces. As shown in the following diagram, the PPC will shift outward.

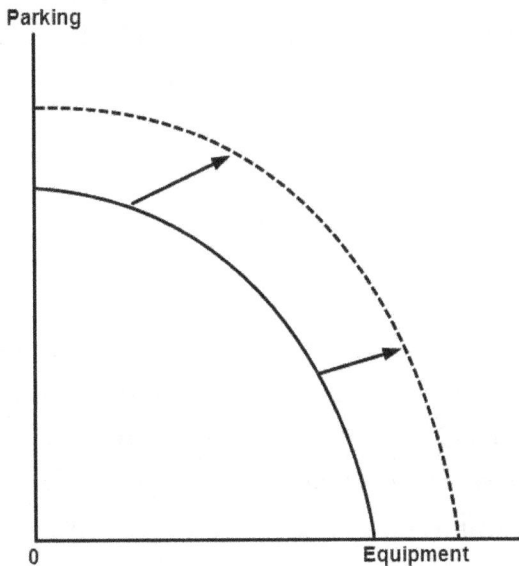

Scenario 12: Not a Drum was heard for the Free Market System

The free market system is not a perfect system, and some of the claims against it are true, but the system does have very important advantages. In a market-oriented economic system, individuals enjoy freedom of choice. Individuals and groups are free to own resources and to use them to advance their own self-interest, thus the system provides incentives for people to pursue their economic objectives and improve their economic well-being as they perceive them. Under a free market economic system, every individual has an opportunity to use his or her talents and resources for his or her own benefit.

Under the free market economic system, the goods and services that consumers want are produced without any deliberate coordinated decision-making. The system works automatically for the most part and is therefore relatively efficient. In such a system, there is no need to make special arrangements with a grocery store to provide you with milk today. If you wanted to, you could go confidently to the grocery store knowing that you could buy the milk you wanted. Under this system, you don't have to make any arrangements with the university cafeteria for your two eggs, toast, coffee, and orange juice on any particular morning, yet you are quite confident that you will be able to obtain breakfast any morning. The system works in such a way that it does not require a great deal of coordination for a market-oriented economy to produce the goods and services that consumers want to buy.

Scenario 13: What is the Question? The Free Market Answers

O.K., Eugene. The "what" problem is what to produce? The economy faces scarcity of resources so it cannot produce all the goods and services that are required to satisfy all human wants. If it produces more cars, it must produce fewer classrooms. Now listen carefully because this is the part that you don't understand. In a free enterprise system, firms engage in production because they hope to make a profit by selling the product at a price that exceeds the cost of production. It follows then, that firms will produce what consumers want to buy. Consumers express their wants by their behavior in the market. Firms respond by producing those goods and services that receive the highest number of dollar votes. Suppose a manufacturing company decides to produce a certain product called *cuties* and then finds out that consumers are unwilling to spend their money on that particular product. The firm will soon discover that the production of *cuties* is not profitable and will put its resources into some other venture. By their decision not to purchase *cuties*, consumers have communicated effectively to the manufacturing company that they do not want *cuties* produced. The free enterprise economic system thus decides "what" to produce.

Scenario 14: Search and You will Find the Circular Flow Model

The diagram is called a *circular flow model*, and we studied it in class just two days ago. Resources (those are the things like labour and land that are used to produce goods and services) flow from the households (people like you and me and our parents and friends) to the factor market. In this market, households sell their resources to firms in exchange for money. You will notice a flow of resources from the factor market to the firms and a flow of money from the factor market to the households.

Now, the firms have the resources and the households have money which is the income they receive from selling their resources. The firms use the resources to produce goods and services (products) that they sell to households in the product market. Notice the flow of goods and services from the firms to the product market and the flow of money from the households to the product market. After the exchange takes place, there is a flow of goods and services (products) from the product market to the households and a flow of money from the product market to the firms.

Scenario 15: Fluctuations in Gas Prices. Demand and Supply Can Explain Them

This document illustrates that fluctuations in gas prices may be due to factors other than price-fixing and collusion by oil companies. Specifically, this analysis shows that the market forces of demand and supply can explain the fluctuations observed in gas prices over the past three years. Four cases are considered.

1. *An increase in demand:* During holidays, the demand for gasoline tends to increase as motorists tend to travel longer distances. In the following graph, the demand curve for gasoline shifts to the right and the equilibrium price rises from P to P1 as shown in the diagram.

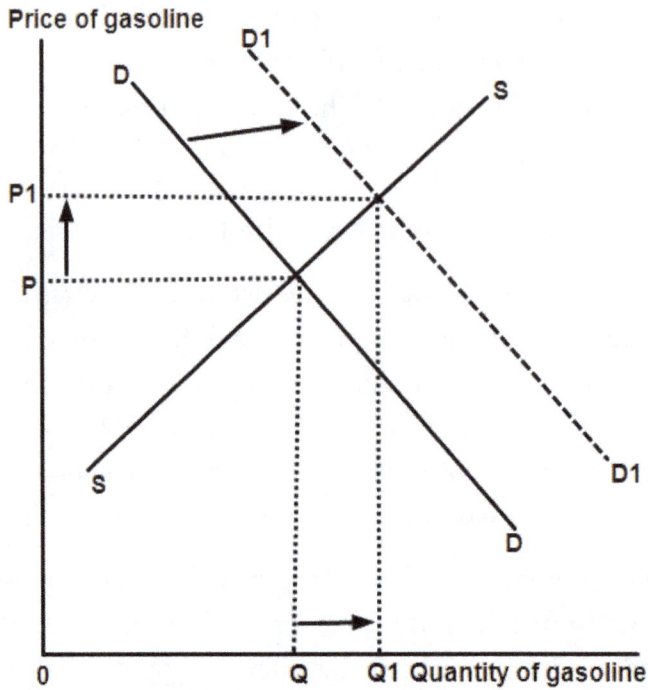

2. *A decrease in demand:* During the winter season and on very cold days, the demand for gasoline tends to decrease as travellers tend to restrict their movements because of the cold. As a result, the demand curve shifts to the left from DD to D0D0, and the price falls from P to P0 as shown.

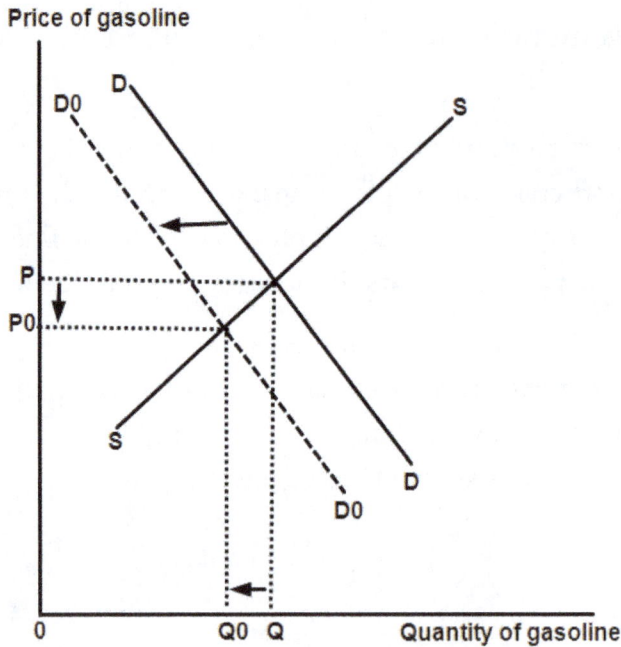

3. *An increase in supply:* Faster extraction of oil increases the supply of gasoline. This causes the supply curve to shift to the right from SS to S1S1 as shown in the diagram, and the price falls from P to P0.

Price of gasoline

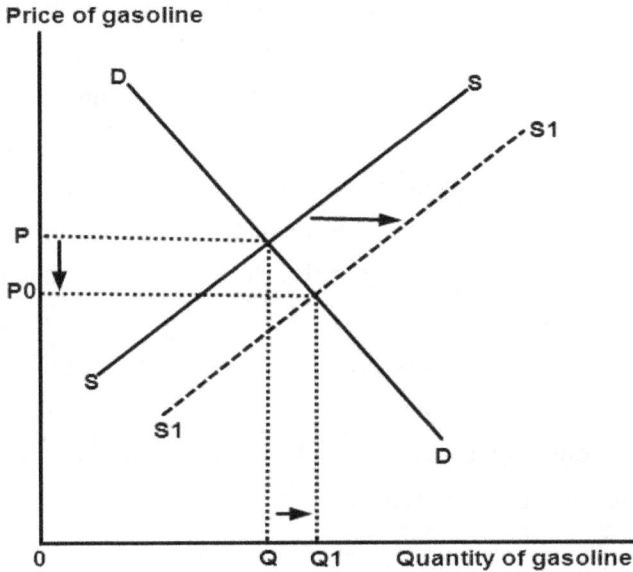

4. *A decrease in supply:* An accidental oilfield fire will reduce the supply of oil and hence the supply of gasoline. As seen in the graph below, the supply curve shifts to the left and the price rises.

Price of gasoline

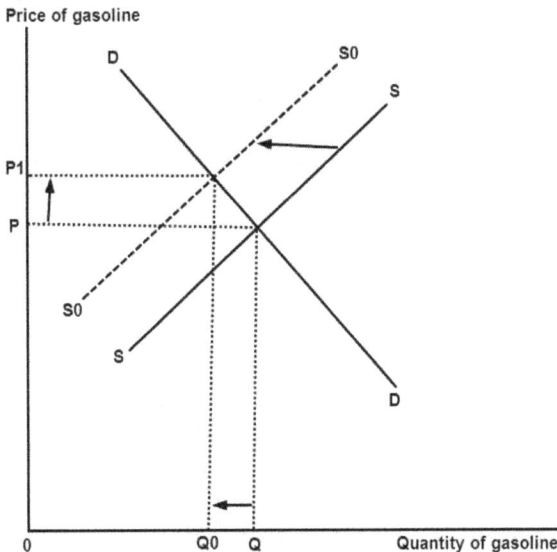

Scenario 16: Review of Residence Pricing Policy at Best Business University

At a price of $2,500 per semester, the quantity of rooms demanded is 115; but BBU can accommodate only 105 students. Thus, BBU's current pricing policy results in a shortage of rooms in its dormitories. The university is charging a price that is too low. A higher price would lower the quantity of rooms demanded and thus get rid of or reduce the shortage. The demand schedule shows that the quantity of rooms demanded and the quantity supplied are equal at 105 rooms, when the rate is $2,700/semester. Thus to clear the market (achieve equilibrium), BBU should increase its rate to $2,700. This increase in the price of its rooms will have no effect on the *demand* for accommodation, but the *quantity demanded* will fall. Accommodation at neighbouring residences must be seen as substitutes for rooms at BBU. Therefore, if neighbouring residences raise their rates, students will switch to the now relatively cheaper rooms at BBU. One would expect the demand for rooms at BBU's dormitories to increase.

Price per room/semester ($)	Quantity of rooms demanded/semester
2,800	100
2,700	105
2,600	110
2,500	115
2,400	120
2,300	125
2,200	130

Scenario 17: Arise and Shine: The Market for Coffee

On the basis of the demand schedule for coffee at Bread of Life Bakery and Café, Violet's intention to charge a price of $4 per package of coffee will not achieve her objective of selling her entire stock and leaving customers not wanting more or less. At that price, she will sell only 1,000 packages, leaving a surplus of 1,000 packages. To accomplish her objective, Violet will have to lower the price to $3.00. At this price, customers will be willing and able to buy the entire stock of 2,000 packages.

The market will be in equilibrium. A similar product at Daily Bread would be considered a substitute for coffee from Bread of Life Bakery and Café. If Daily Bread increases the price of its coffee, customers will switch to Bread of Life so the demand for coffee from Bread of Life will increase. On the other hand, if Daily Bread reduces its price, the demand for the product from Bread of Life will fall as customers switch from Bread of Life to Daily Bread whose price would now be cheaper.

Scenario 18: The Politics and Economics of Minimum Wage Legislation

In many (if not most) jurisdictions, minimum wage legislation is a fact of life. The stated purpose of such legislation is to ensure that workers earn a decent wage and that employers do not take unfair advantage of employees. This document analyzes the economic effects of minimum wage legislation.

The following graph of the labour market will help to illustrate the argument. The demand curve for labour is **DL** and the supply curve is **SL**. The market equilibrium wage rate is determined by the intersection of the demand and supply curves. This equilibrium wage rate is indicated by **We**. At this wage rate, the quantity of labour demanded is **L** and the quantity supplied is also **L**. There is no surplus or shortage of workers.

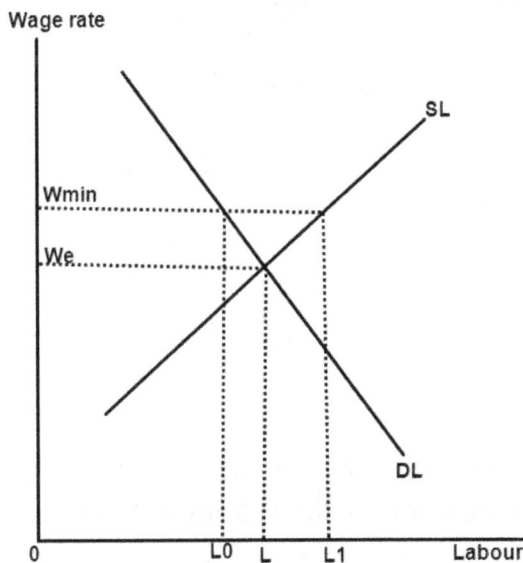

If the minimum wage is set below the market equilibrium of **We**, it will have no effect. The equilibrium wage rate will prevail. However, if the minimum wage is set above the market equilibrium wage, such as **Wmin** in the diagram, the number of workers that will be hired by employers will be **L0**, while the number of workers seeking employment will be **L1**. Thus, the number of workers who will not be hired is (**L1 − L0**). This represents unemployment that it due to the minimum wage legislation.

Scenario 19: Rent Control to the Rescue? A Better Way?

a) Let us consider the market for rental units. The demand for rental units is shown by the curve DD in the diagram, and the supply is shown by the curve SS. The market equilibrium rent is $700 per month and at that price, 1,700 units are demanded (rented) and supplied. In other words, the market clears at that price.

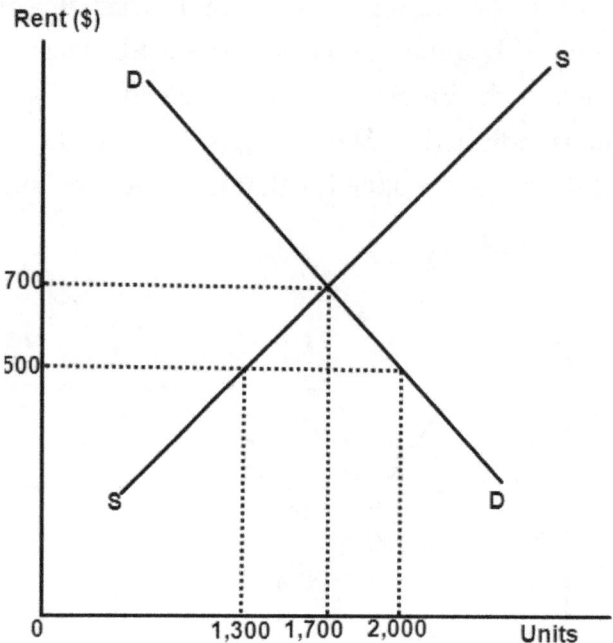

Now, suppose the Rent Control Board decides to limit rent to $500 per month. At this price, the quantity demanded jumps to 2,000 units while the quantity supplied falls to 1,300 units. The action of the Rent Control Board has created a shortage of rental units of (2,000 − 1,300) = 700. At the administered price of $500 a month, landlords may not have any incentives to maintain their buildings. Needed repairs are left undone, and the buildings begin to deteriorate—the development of slums.

b) If the city considers rent to be too high at $700 per month, one alternative to rent control would be to provide incentives such as tax breaks to developers to increase the supply of rental units. Also, the city could enter the housing market and build affordable rental units. Such measures would shift the supply curve to the right and reduce the rent.

Scenario 20: Farmers on the Move. Quotas and All That

a) Significant increases in the productivity of farmers over the years have increased the supply of farm products, thus lowering their prices. As the prices of farm products fall, the quantity demanded does not increase much. There is only so much food that people can eat. The incomes of farmers therefore do not increase significantly. When incomes in the society increase, the demand for most goods and services also increases. However, the increase in demand for farm products does not keep pace with the increase in demand for other goods and services, so farmers do not benefit as much as the rest of society.

b) The imposition of a quota on farm products raises the prices of farm products. It is possible for this increase in the prices of farm products to improve the well-being of farmers. The following diagram of the market for farm products will help to illustrate the idea.

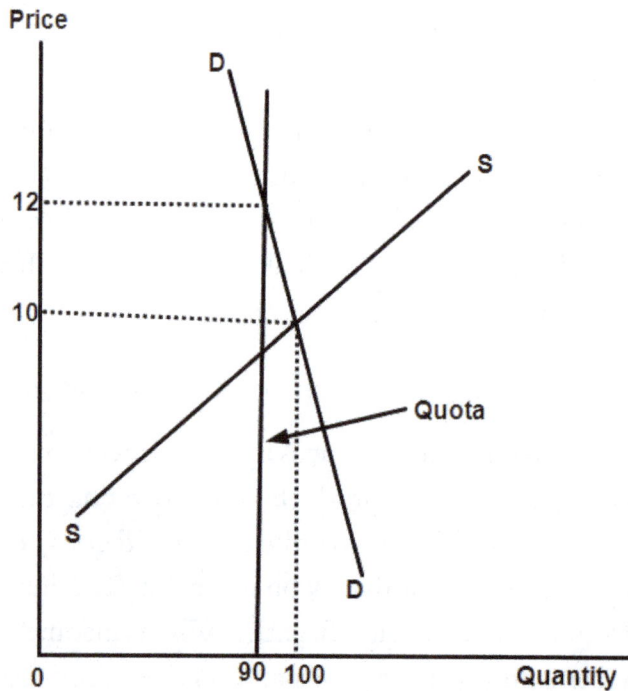

The demand and supply for farm products is shown by DD and SS respectively. The steepness of the DD curve implies that changes in the prices of farm products do not meaningfully affect the quantity demanded. The equilibrium price is $10 and the equilibrium quantity is 100. Farm income is therefore ($10 × 100) = $1,000.

Now, suppose the quota is set at 90, which is 10% less than the equilibrium quantity of 100. If the price rises by 20% as a result of the fall in supply, the price will rise from $10 to $12. Farm income will now be ($12 × 90) = $1,080. In this case, the quota increases farm income by $80.

Scenario 21: Here Comes Professor Noce. Beware of False Demand and Supply Doctrines

There are several errors and misunderstandings in the professor's responses. First, it should be noted that an increase in the demand for laptops cannot be the result of a fall in their prices. A fall in the price of laptop computers will lead to an increase in the quantity of laptop computers demanded, not to an increase in demand. Contrary to Professor Noce's assertion, the law of demand states that if the price of an item falls, other things being equal, the quantity demanded will rise, and vice versa.

Second, when asked what happens to price when demand increases, the professor declared that he was not sure. His explanation was that when demand increases, price rises, and when price rises, demand falls. The fall in demand will lower the price. So the effect of an increase in demand on price is ambiguous. The professor is wrong. When demand increases, other things being equal, price will rise. When price rises, the quantity demanded (not demand) falls. The professor confused demand and quantity demanded.

Third, the professor's response to the question regarding complementary goods is hilarious. Simply stated, complementary goods are goods that are used together. Computers and USB flash drives are complementary goods; so are automobiles and tires, and chalk and chalk board.

Finally, supply and demand are related but certainly not in the sense that the professor explains it. Actually, when demand increases, nothing happens to supply as a result, but the quantity supplied does increase; and when supply increases, nothing happens to demand as a result, but the quantity supplied does increase.

Scenario 22: Sally's Dilemma—Math to the Rescue

The demand for and supply of Sally's bags is as follows:

$Qd = 130 - 3P$

$Qs = 100$

For the market (in this case Sally's) to clear, the quantity of bags demanded must be equal to the quantity supplied. Therefore,

$130 - 3P = 100$

$$-3P = -30$$

$$P = 10$$

Sally should charge **$10** for her bags.

Now, if the demand for her bags increases by 15, the demand equation will become

$Qd = (130 + 15) - 3P$, and the supply equation will remain unchanged at $= 100$

For the market to clear (neither a shortage nor a shortage), the quantity demanded and the quantity supplied must be equal. Thus:

$(130 + 15) - 3P = 100$

$145 - 3P = 100$

$\quad - 3P = -45$

$\quad\quad P = 15$

Sally should increase the price of her bags from $10 to **$15**.

Scenario 23: Jorobel Revisited. National Income Accounting

Jorobel's GDP

Income method

It is assumed that there is no depreciation of capital and no indirect business taxes.

Item Value ($million)

Profits (π)	120
Rental income (R)	250
Wages (W)	1,100
Interest and dividends (i)	70

$GDP = W + R + i + \pi = 1{,}100 + 250 + 70 + 120 = \mathbf{1{,}540}$

Expenditure method

Item Value ($million)

Consumption expenditure (C)	800
Gross investment (Ig)	420
Government purchases (G)	300
Exports (X)	160
Imports (M)	140

$GDP = C + I + G + (X - M) = 800 + 420 + 300 + (160 - 140) = \mathbf{1{,}540}$

Petilonia's GDP

From the available data, the income method can be used to calculate Petilonia's GDP.

GDP income based $= W + R + i + \pi + D + T_{IB} = 200 + 10 + 60 + 20 + 30 + 40 + 20 = 380$

GDP = $380 million

Recall that gross investment (I_G) = net investment (I_N) + D

GDP expenditure based = C + I_G + G + (X − M) = 240 + (30 + 40) + G + (6 − 5) = 311 + G

But GDP = $380 million from the income method; therefore G = 380 − 311 = 69

Government spending on goods and services = **$69 million**.

Scenario 24: Where are the Jobs?

There are several reasons why people are unemployed. First, in a free enterprise system where workers are free to quit their jobs and where employers are free to terminate the employment of workers, unemployment is unavoidable. It will often take some time for new entrants into the labour force (new graduates, for example) to find work, and it also takes time for a discharged worker to find another job. This cause of unemployment is referred to as *frictional unemployment* and is consistent with the functioning of a market economy. There will always be frictional unemployment in the economy.

Frictional unemployment is not the only type of unemployment that the economy experiences. The economy is subject to fluctuations in GDP. When the economy is contracting, firms are producing less and do not need as many workers, so unemployment results. This type of unemployment is referred to as *cyclical unemployment*. Moreover, unemployment may be caused by structural changes that take place in the economy. Tastes change and the demand for goods and services changes consequently. As industries decline, people lose their jobs and may have difficulty finding new ones. This type of unemployment is referred to as *structural unemployment*. Finally, there is *seasonal unemployment* that is due to seasonal variations. For example, certain economic activities slow down or come to a halt in countries that experience a winter season, and this results in unemployment.

Scenario 25: Unemployment is Costly

The GDP gap—the difference between potential GDP and actual GDP—is a good measure of the economic cost of unemployment. Using Okun's law with a ratio of 2.5, we can use the following formula to estimate the economic cost of unemployment in Okunia.

GDP gap = 2.5 × cyclical unemployment × GDP

GDP gap = 2.5 × 9.4% × \$115 billion ≈ \$27.03 billion.

This means that Okunia loses about \$27.03 billion worth of goods and services because of unemployment.

Scenario 26: The Varieties of Unemployment

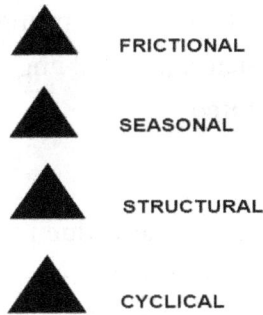

TYPES

OF

UNEMPLOYMENT

▲ FRICTIONAL

▲ SEASONAL

▲ STRUCTURAL

▲ CYCLICAL

Department of Labour: Laboria

Introduction

Unemployment is an economic problem with which the Government of Laboria is deeply concerned. In this pamphlet we present the various types of unemployment so that you will be better informed about this particular economic problem. Unemployment is a state of joblessness. It can reap havoc on the unemployed, their families, and on the economy as a whole. The unemployed are those members of the adult population who are actively looking and available for work. Let us look at the various types of unemployment and what may be done to reduce them.

Frictional Unemployment

In an economic system such as that of Laboria, where people are free to change their jobs and in which employers are free to dismiss workers for just cause, such as inefficiency and redundancy, frictional unemployment is unavoidable. This type of unemployment results from people leaving jobs before they have another one lined up, or people entering the labour force for the first time. This type of unemployment can be reduced to some extent by providing better information about job opportunities and available workers, and by manpower planning. However, it is not possible to completely eliminate frictional unemployment.

Seasonal Unemployment

Seasonal unemployment is unemployment that results from seasonal variations. In a country like Laboria where seasonal differences are pronounced, seasonal unemployment is common and expected. In the cold and snowy months, agricultural activities slow down and unemployment in this sector increases. Construction activities also slow down and unemployment increases in this sector. In the summer months, unemployment increases among people whose jobs are related to winter activities such as ice skating, and skiing. The scope of policies to deal with seasonal unemployment is limited.

Structural Unemployment

Structural unemployment is unemployment that is due to structural changes in the economy. Changes in demand patters and in techniques in production may result in unemployment. A permanent decline in the demand for textiles, for example, will cause unemployment in the textile and related industries. The introduction of labour-saving technology in many industries has resulted in structural unemployment. Structural unemployment can be reduced by providing retraining for those whose skills are no longer in demand.

Cyclical Unemployment

A deficiency in total spending in an economy may result in economic slowdown that results in unemployment. This is the type of unemployment referred to as *cyclical unemployment*. A market economy like the economy of Laboria, periodically goes through ups and downs known as business cycles. When the economy is on the upswing, unemployment tends to fall, and when it is on the downswing, unemployment tends to rise. Fiscal policy and monetary policy can be used to reduce this type of unemployment.

Scenario 27: Recover Lost Labour Market Data

	January	February	March	April
Adult population	200	200	220	220
Not in labour force	80	**90**	90	90
Labour force	**120**	110	**130**	**130**
Employed	100	**100**	100	110
Unemployed	20	10	30	20
Unemployment rate (%)	16.7	9.1	23.1	15.4
Labour force participation rate (%)	60.0	55.0	59.1	59.1

Not in labour force (February)

The adult population consists of those in the labour force plus those who are not in the labour force. In February, the adult population was 200 of which 110 were in the labour force. Therefore, the number not in the labour force was (200 – 110) = 90.

Labour force (January)

The adult population of 200 in January consisted of those who were not in the labour force (80) plus those in the labour force; thus labour force = (200 – 80) = 120.

Labour force (March)

The labour force is the adult population less those who are not in the labour force. That is (220 – 90) = 130.

Labour force (April)

The labour force is the adult population less those who are not in the labour force. That is (220 – 90) = 130.

Employed (February)

The labour force consists of the employed plus the unemployed. The labour force = 110, unemployed = 10, therefore the employed is (110 – 10) = 100.

Employed (March)

The labour force = 130, unemployed = 30, therefore the employed = (130 − 30) = 100.

Employed (April)

The labour force = 130, unemployed = 20, therefore the employed = (130 − 20) = 110.

Unemployed (January)

The labour force is 120, employed = 100, therefore unemployed = (120 − 100) = 20

$$\text{The unemployment rate is } \frac{\text{Unemployed}}{\text{Labour force}} \times 100$$

Unemployment rate (January): $\frac{20}{120} \times 100 =$ **16.7**

Unemployment rate (February): $\frac{10}{110} \times 100 =$ **9.1**

Unemployment rate (March): $\frac{30}{130} \times 100 =$ **23.1**

Unemployment rate (April): $\frac{20}{130} \times 100 =$ **15.4**

$$\text{The labour force participation rate is } \frac{\text{Labour force}}{\text{Adult population}} \times 100$$

$$\text{Participation rate (January): } \frac{120}{200} \times 100 = \mathbf{60.0}$$

$$\text{Participation rate (February): } \frac{110}{200} \times 100 = \mathbf{55.0}$$

$$\text{Participation rate (March): } \frac{130}{220} \times 100 = \mathbf{59.1}$$

$$\text{Participation rate (April): } \frac{130}{220} \times 100 = \mathbf{59.1}$$

Scenario 28: The *Real* Crux of the Matter at Fairlee. Don't Forget the Cost of Living

We should not be fooled by the offer of a 4% increase in our pay. It may sound good on the surface but we must examine it more carefully. Let's say that a worker is earning $20.00 an hour. An increase of 4% would bring his pay up to $20.80 per hour, so for a 40-hour week, his salary increases from $800.00 to $832.00. To get to the real crux of the matter, we have to look beyond the face value of our pay and focus on the real value. That is, we must look at the purchasing power of our pay—how much we can buy with it. At a 6% rate of inflation, the real purchasing power of the $832.00 turns out to be only $782.08. By accepting an offer of 4% increase in our pay when the rate of inflation is 6%, we are actually falling behind. The real crux of the matter is that just to maintain our purchasing power (that is, our real income), we would need an increase of 6%.

Scenario 29: Will the Real GDP Please Stand Up?

There are several reasons that may explain the phenomenon in Battanovia. First, the official GDP figures include, for the most part, only those goods and services that are produced and sold in regular, recognized markets. For this reason, many goods and services that are actually produced in the Battanovian economy do not get counted in the official GDP estimates. Included in this category are volunteer work, housework and garage chores, and vegetables produced in home gardens.

Second, a fair amount of goods and services are produced in what is called the underground or cash economy but they do not get counted in the official GDP statistics. Economic activities such as gambling, prostitution, and drug trafficking are not fully accounted for in the official, reported GDP. To this must be added transactions such as driveway paving, babysitting, home repairs, auto repairs, medical and legal services that are paid for in cash and are not reported.

Scenario 30: The Reluctant Philosophers. Effects of Inflation

Inflation is like a two-winged eagle enriching one group while impoverishing another. Bob most likely belongs to the group that benefits from inflation while Tom belongs to the group that is hurt by inflation. It would not at all be surprising to find out that Bob is a debtor who will benefit by repaying his debt with money whose value has fallen. It might also be that Bob is involved in some kind of business where the prices of the goods and services sold rises faster than the cost of producing those goods and services, resulting in an increase in profits. These are reasons why Bob might be delighted that the rate of inflation has increased.

Tom, on the other hand, is most likely among those on fixed incomes. It would not be surprising if he has some funds in a savings account. That money loses purchasing power in the presence of inflation. He has probably lent money to some people and realizes that when he is repaid, the money will have lost some value because of inflation. No wonder then that Tom is disappointed to learn of the increase in the rate of inflation.

Scenario 31: Not the Boston Tea Party; Some Protection from Inflation

The outspoken woman's assertion about the damaging effects of inflation cannot be meaningfully denied, but we are not helpless victims without recourse. We can do something to protect ourselves from inflation. For example, we know that lenders (creditors) lose during an inflation because when they are repaid, the money they receive will have lost some purchasing power. Creditors can protect themselves from this potential loss by charging a rate of interest that takes the rate of inflation into consideration. Consider another example. We know that during an inflation, the values of real assets such as valuable antique, art, or coins rise, whereas the values of financial assets such as savings accounts and bonds fall. This suggests that we can protect ourselves from the ravages of inflation, to some extent, by switching our assets out of financial assets into real estate, for example. By using our savings to purchase real assets, we could actually benefit from inflation.

Scenario 32: Fiscal Policy to the Rescue

The economic cost of unemployment can be measured by the GDP gap. According to Okun's law, we can calculate the GDP gap by using the following formula:

GDP gap = 2.5 × cyclical unemployment (%) × GDP

That is, GDP gap = 2.5 × 4.2% × $1506.83 billion = **$158.2 billion.**

Thus we can conclude that the economic cost of unemployment in Recessia is **$158.2 billion**.

In this case, there is a recessionary gap. In order to reduce or eliminate this gap, the Government of Recessia can adopt an expansionary fiscal policy. This policy entails an increase in government spending and/or a reduction in taxes. The increase in government spending ($\Delta G\uparrow$) will cause an increase in income ($\Delta Y\uparrow$) which will lead to an increase in consumption ($\Delta C\uparrow$). As consumption increases, producers will spend more in order to meet the increased demand from consumers, thus causing an increase in investment ($\Delta I\uparrow$). The increase in spending by the government, consumers and firms represents an increase in aggregate expenditure ($\Delta AE\uparrow$) which stimulates the economy and moves it towards the full-employment level of output. Symbolically:

$$\Delta G\uparrow \rightarrow \Delta Y\uparrow \rightarrow \Delta C\uparrow \rightarrow \Delta I\uparrow \rightarrow \Delta AE\uparrow$$

A reduction in taxes ($\Delta T\downarrow$) will increase disposable income ($\Delta Yd\uparrow$), increase consumption and investment and stimulate the economy, moving it towards potential real GDP.

The following diagram illustrates how this policy will work.

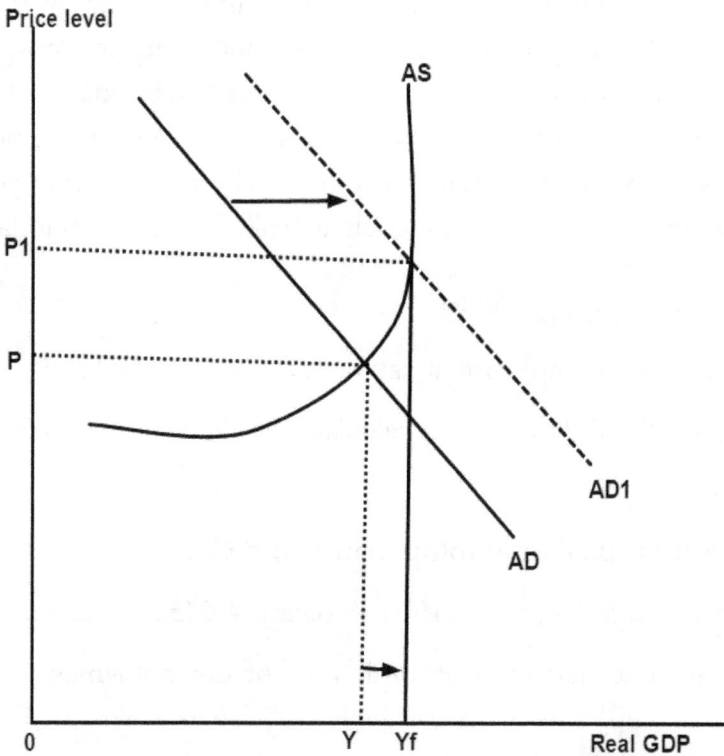

The economy is initially in equilibrium with a real GDP of Y and a price level of P. Yf is potential real GDP. To eliminate the gap between Yf and Y, and thus move the economy from Y to Yf, the government can increase its spending and reduce taxes. Such a policy would shift the AD curve to the right from AD to AD1, and the economy would be in equilibrium at the potential level of real GDP with a price level of P1, which is exactly what the policy is designed to do.

During a period of inflation, there is an inflationary gap. In order to reduce or eliminate this gap, the government can implement a contractionary fiscal policy.

This policy entails a decrease in government spending and/or an increase in taxes. The following diagram illustrates how this policy will work.

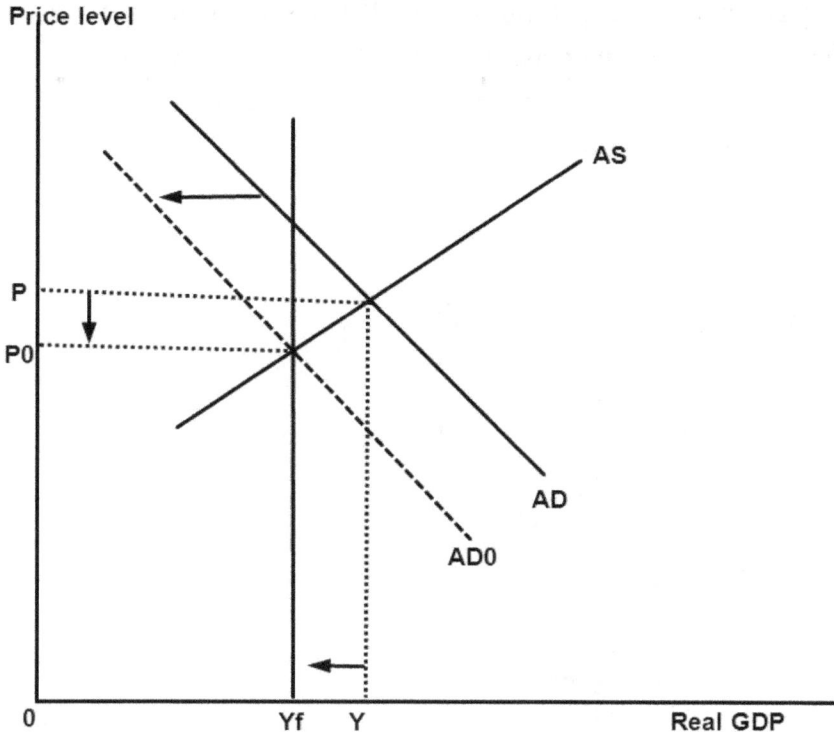

Price level

```
                                              AS

P ........................
PO .................

                                         AD

                              AD0

0              Yf   Y                Real GDP
```

The economy is initially at equilibrium with a real GDP of Y and a price level of P. But this equilibrium is above potential GDP (Yf) so there is an inflationary gap. To eliminate the gap between Y and Yf, and thus move the economy from Y to Yf, the Government of Recessia can reduce its spending and raise taxes. Such a policy would shift the AD curve to the left from AD to AD0, and the economy would be in equilibrium at the potential level of real GDP with a price level of P0, thus eliminating the gap.

Scenario 33: AD/AS? Show Me in Pictures

a) *Effect of an increase in investment spending*

The economy is initially in equilibrium in the Keynesian range with a real GDP of Y and a price level of P. An increase in investment spending will increase aggregate expenditure and therefore shift the AD curve to the right from AD to AD1 as shown in the following diagram.

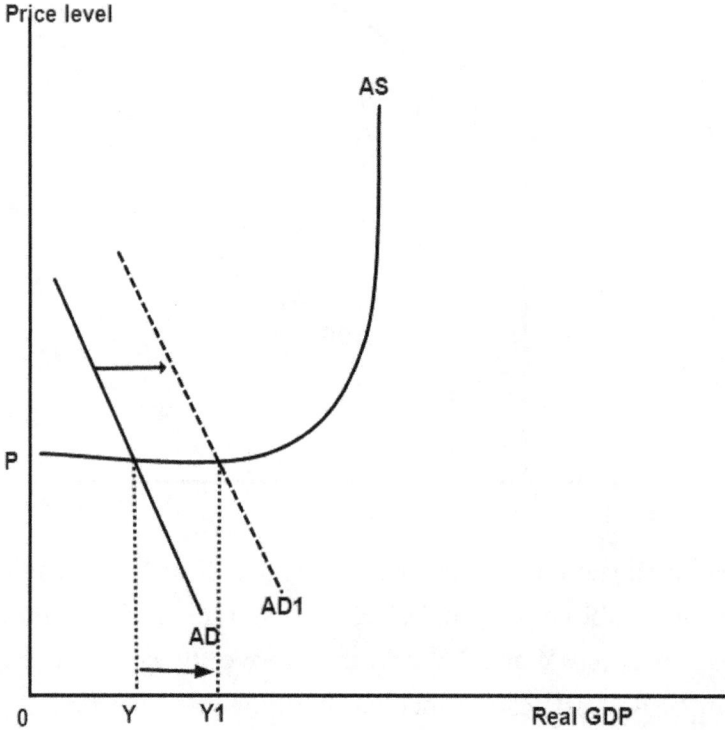

As a result, real GDP increases from Y to Y1, but the price level remains unchanged at P.

b) *Effects of rapid and prolonged increases in the price of oil*

The economy is in equilibrium in the intermediate range at a price level of P and a real GDP of Y as shown in the following diagram.

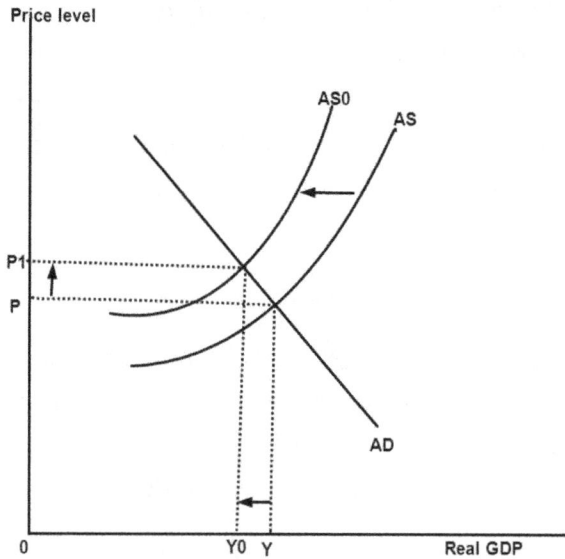

Rapid and prolonged increases in the price of oil will drive up the costs of production and shift the AS curve to the left from AS to AS0 as shown in the diagram. This decrease in aggregate supply raises the price level from P to P1 and reduces real GDP from Y to Y0.

c) *Effects of a contractionary fiscal policy*

The following diagram shows that the economy is in equilibrium with a price level of P and a real GDP of Y.

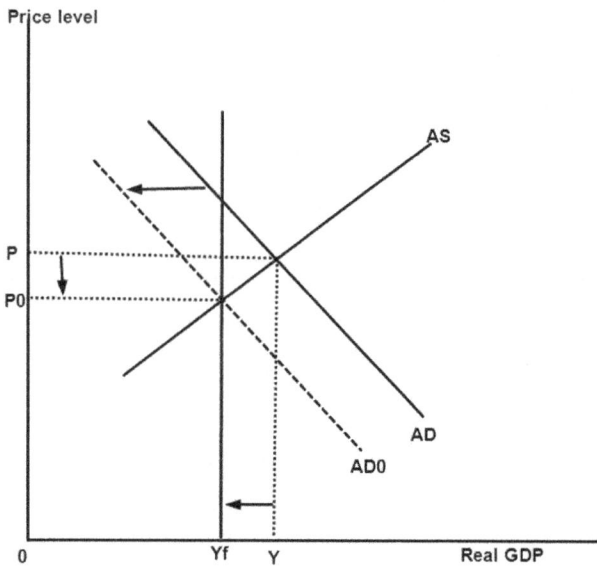

A contractionary fiscal policy involving a decrease in government spending and/or an increase in taxes will reduce aggregate expenditure and shift the AD curve from AD to AD0 as shown in the diagram. This decrease in aggregate demand will lower the equilibrium price level from P to P0, and reduce the equilibrium level of real GDP from Y to the full employment level of Yf, thus eliminating the inflationary gap.

d) *Effects of an economy-wide training program*

In the following diagram, P and Y represent the initial equilibrium price level and equilibrium real GDP respectively. An economy-wide training program will increase the productivity of labour and therefore shift the aggregate supply curve to the right from AS to AS1 as shown in the diagram.

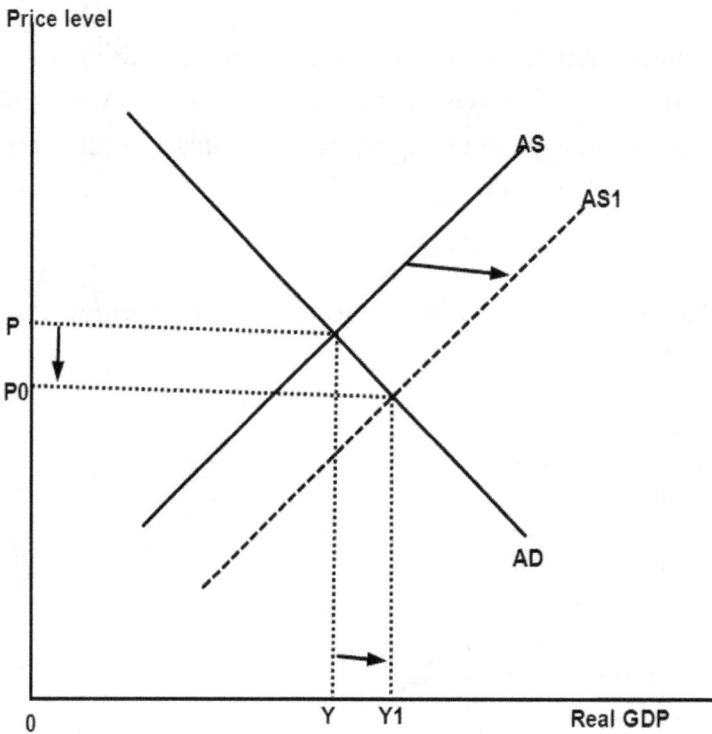

As a result, the equilibrium price level falls from P to P0, and the equilibrium real GDP increases from Y to Y1.

e) Effects of an increase in consumer wealth when the economy is operating at potential GDP

The following diagram shows the economy in equilibrium at Yf, the potential GDP, with a price level of P.

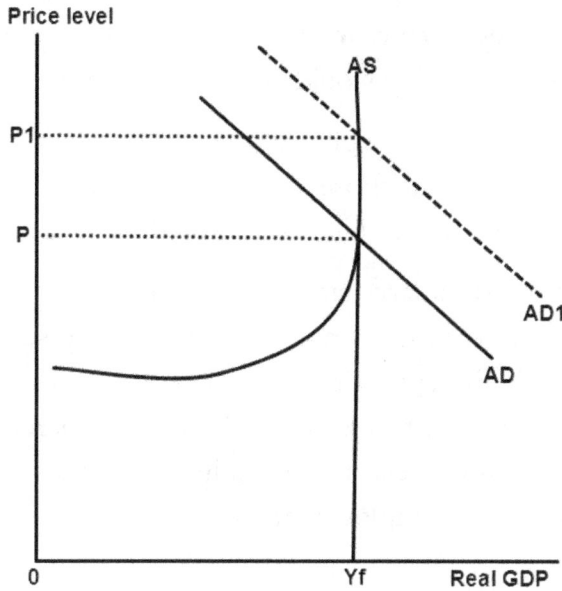

An increase in consumer wealth will cause an increase in consumer spending that will shift the aggregate demand curve from AD to AD1 as shown in the diagram. Since the economy is operating at its potential GDP, the increase in aggregate demand has no effect on real GDP, but it causes the equilibrium price level to rise from P to P1.

Scenario 34: Professor Charle A. Tan Lectures on Fiscal Policy

Inaccuracies in Professor Charle A. Tan's Lecture

First, fiscal policy does deal with finance and money, but it is not at all as the professor defines it, and it is not conducted by the central bank. In fact, fiscal policy refers to changes in government spending and taxes and is clearly conducted by the government and not the central bank. What the good professor defined as fiscal policy is actually monetary policy.

Second, Professor Charle. A. Tan says that "Whenever interest rates change, you know that the central bank is conducting fiscal policy." This is erroneous. Changes in interest rates may not be indicative of any kind of policy. For example, if consumers and firms borrow more money, other things being equal, interest rates will rise and this has nothing to do with economic policy of any kind.

Third, in his prescription for unemployment and low output, Professor Charle A. Tan continues to be confused about fiscal policy. Moreover, if the central bank were to reduce the money supply, interest rates would rise, yes, but consumer spending and investment spending would fall and worsen the economic situation.

Fourth, the professor's claim that higher interest rates would encourage saving is true, but it does not follow that those savings will be borrowed by firms to be channelled into investment. Higher interest rates reduce investment spending.

Fifth, Professor Tan's summary simply reiterates the inaccuracies already mentioned. In fact, whenever the economy is experiencing severe unemployment and low levels of GDP, the appropriate fiscal policy is for the government to increase its spending and reduce taxes. This will lead to an increase in income which will generate consumer and investment spending, and thus stimulate economic activity, increasing output and employment.

Scenario 35: It's a Roller Coaster. No. It's Sea Waves? No. It's the Business Cycle

It represents ups and downs in economic activity. Economists refer to it as the *business cycle*. The upward-sloping straight line shows the general upward trend in the economy through time. As time progresses, the economy produces more goods and services. However, the total quantity of all goods and services that the economy produces (we refer to it as the real GDP) fluctuates as shown in the diagram. You will notice that all the high points are referred to as *peaks*. At such high points, the economy has reached its highest level. For a variety of reasons (Prof says we will study them later), the peak ends and a recession begins. A *recession* is a general downturn in economic activity. In this phase of the business cycle, consumers' incomes are declining so they spend less money buying stuff. Also, businesses invest less and hire fewer workers so unemployment increases. This is definitely not a happy time for most people. This general decline in economic activity sooner or later hits bottom—a phase referred to as a trough. The *trough* is the lowest point of the business cycle. In this phase, unemployment is high, real GDP has fallen, and in general, people are spending less than previously. This too will end and the economy then enters the phase called the *recovery* or *expansion*. During this phase, employment and income increase, firms are optimistic about the economy and are investing and producing more. The GDP is growing again until it reaches the peak, after which we start all over again.

Scenario 36: Study Group in Economics: Sharing the Work on the Business Cycle—Multiplier-Accelerator

I think it is easier to understand the multiplier-accelerator theory of the business cycle if we first understand the acceleration principle. The acceleration principle or simply, the accelerator, is closely associated with the concept of induced investment which we learned earlier. The principle of acceleration states that an increase in income leads to an accelerated increase in investment.

The following table illustrates the operation of this principle.

Required

Year	Total output ($000)	capital stock ($000)	Investment ($000)
1	50	200	0
2	52	208	8
3	52	208	0
4	54	216	8
5	56	224	8
6	58	232	8
7	59	236	4
8	62	248	12
9	66	264	16
10	70	280	16

Assume that there is no depreciation of capital. Therefore, there is no difference between gross investment and net investment. Let us assume that it takes $4 worth of capital to produce $1 output per year. In other words, the capital-output ratio (that is, the ratio of the value of capital to total output) is assumed to be 4:1.

Let us focus on the table. It shows that an annual output of $50,000 requires a capital stock of $200,000. An increase in output of $2,000 in year 2 requires an increase in the capital stock from $200,000 to $208,000—that is, an investment of $8,000. The table shows that if output increases at a constant rate (as in years 4 to 6), investment will remain at a constant level. If the rate of increase in output falls off (as from year 6 to 7), investment will fall. Investment will increase when total output rises at an increasing rate as in years 7 to 9. You will notice that investment is proportional to the change in total output. Given the change in total output, the amount of investment required can be calculated by multiplying the change in output by the capital-output ratio or the accelerator.

The formula for the required investment can be developed by using simple algebra.

K = required capital stock

Y = total output

Let $K/Y = v$, where v is constant

Then $K = vY$

$\Delta K = v\Delta Y$

That is, $I = v\Delta Y$ where I is the required investment.

Since Vince has asked for an example of how the formula may be used, here is an example.

Example. Suppose you know that the capital-output ratio is 4. How much investment is required to increase output from $56 million to $58 million?

Solution.

$K/Y = v = 4; \Delta Y = 2,000,000$

But $I = v\Delta Y$

Therefore, $I = 4 \times 2,000,000 = \$8,000,000$

The required investment is $8,000,000

Let us proceed to the role of the accelerator in business cycles. Paul Samuelson demonstrated that the interaction of the multiplier and the accelerator can produce wide fluctuations in economic activity. If the economy is expanding, the increase in income accelerates investment. The increased investment generates an even greater increase in income. But as the economy's resources become fully employed, the acceleration of output slows down. And, as we know, a deceleration in output hinders investment. The decreased investment causes an even greater reduction in output via the multiplier. Hence, the interaction of the multiplier and the accelerator acts to intensify fluctuations in economic activity.

Scenario 37: Professor Noce Comments on Unemployment

Professor Noce's assertion that unemployment exists because people cannot find jobs is stating the obvious. If anyone who wanted a job could find one, then everyone in the labour force would be employed and there would be no unemployment. The rest of the professor's comment seems to make very little sense and demonstrates a serious lack of understanding of the problem of unemployment and the cost that it imposes on the economy. The fact is, because of unemployment, the economy produces a smaller volume of goods and services than would be the case if it were operating at full employment.

The loss of output (that is, the economic cost of unemployment) can be illustrated by the following diagram.

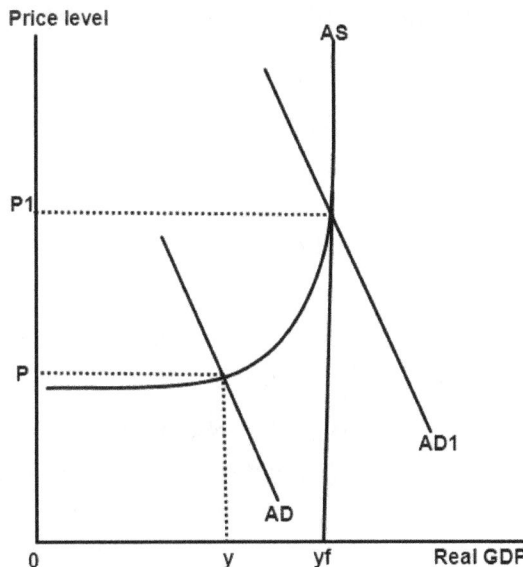

In the diagram, the full-employment level of real GDP, also called potential real GDP, is illustrated as **yf**. However, because of unemployment, the actual output of goods and services produced by the economy is **y**. Thus, the economy is operating below its potential. The difference between yf and y represents the economic cost of unemployment—lost output because of unemployment. Apparently, Professor Noce could benefit from a macroeconomics course at Such University of Economic Science (SUES).

Scenario 38: You Had a Dream—A Conference of Schools of Thought

Reflection on Dream

I don't dream often, and when I do, I don't generally remember the details of any dream. This time was different. I remembered every detail. I reflect particularly on the following:

1. There seems to be a common theme among the Classical, Neoclassical, and New Classical schools of thought—reliance on the market system and quick economic adjustment.
2. The 'K' people and the New Keynesian Schools also seem to have a common theme—sticky prices and wages, and the view that deliberate action by government may be needed to move the economy to some desired position.
3. It's interesting that there are so many different schools of thought in macroeconomics. It suggests that the economy may not be as simple as it may first appear.

Scenario 39: Let the Inventories Speak. Their Role in Output Planning

Inventories do "speak" to producers about the need to vary output to suit demand. Firms keep a certain amount of inventory to meet unanticipated changes in demand. If inventories rise above their intended or planned levels, then the firms' production levels are too high for the current level of demand. An unplanned accumulation of inventories is therefore a signal to producers to reduce their volume of output. The inventories are saying, "We are too much, cut production levels."

On the other hand, if inventories fall below their intended levels, then the firm's production levels are too low for the current level of demand. This situation would be a signal to the firms to increase their volume of output. The inventories are saying, "We are not enough, increase production levels." Unintended changes in inventories thus serve as a barometer that the firms may use to adjust their output to the appropriate level.

Scenario 40: To Be (in equilibrium) or Not to Be? That Is the Question

It is likely that Emma was thinking about Steve's concept of saving and investment, and his failure to indicate explicitly the assumptions that he was making about the economy. His point of view is correct only under certain simplifying assumptions which were not stated, and only if his statement refers to *ex ante* (planned) saving and investment. In an *ex post* (realized) sense, saving and investment must always be equal. Saving, by definition, is the part of income that is not spent on current consumption. Investment is the unconsumed part of current output. In this sense, saving and investment are one and the same thing. Their equality does not define equilibrium income.

Another point is worth mentioning. If we are dealing with an economy where government neither spends nor taxes, and that does not engage in foreign trade, then Steve's assertion is true. The problem is that Steve did not make those assumptions explicit. If we are dealing with an open economy with government spending and taxing, then Steve is incorrect. In such an economy, total injections and total withdrawals may not be equal even if saving and investment are equal. The economy may not be in equilibrium. For an open economy with government spending and taxing to be in equilibrium, the following condition must hold:

$$I + G + X = S + T + M$$

where I = investment, G = government purchases, X = exports, S = saving, T = taxes, and M = imports. Clearly, this does not require saving and investment to be equal.

Scenario 41: Algebra Can Help Even When Two Things Seem Different Because Equilibrium Income Is Equilibrium Income, No Matter How It Looks

Eugene and Cathy have made a good decision to study together. Study groups can be quite effective in learning. Now let's turn our attention to the issue at hand. Indeed, equilibrium income **is** equilibrium income, no matter how the condition is expressed. Assuming a closed economy (no exports or imports) with neither government spending nor taxes, and using the injections-withdrawals approach, equilibrium can be expressed as S (saving) = I (investment). Saving is the withdrawal while investment is the injection. Using the aggregate expenditure (AE)-aggregate output (AO) approach, equilibrium can be expressed as Y = C + I. Since each approach expresses equilibrium under the same circumstances, both approaches are equivalent. Let us begin with,

$$Y = C + I$$

By transposing C, we obtain

$$Y - C = I$$

But $Y - C = S$ by definition

Therefore $S = I$

Thus we see that $Y = C + I$ is identical to $S = I$.

Professor Query was right. It is a simple matter.

Scenario 42: The Public Debt—The Real Burden

The argument raised in the newspaper article is one that I have heard often enough. Until I studied the issue in my macroeconomics course, the argument seemed valid. But the idea of the burden of the public debt being passed on to future generations is a misconception. The public debt is the amount of money that the government owes its creditors. An external debt does transfer a burden from the present to the future. If a country increases its present command over goods and services by borrowing externally, the citizens of the future will have to sacrifice some goods and services when payment is made on the loan. Thus, the burden is passed on to them.

An internal debt, however, is a different matter—a different kettle of fish, if you wish. It does not transfer a burden from the present to the future. It is true that future generations will pay higher taxes because of the loan. But it is equally true that the repayment of the loan is received by future generations. The real burden of an internal debt is not passed on to future generations. It is borne by those individuals who have given up current consumption of goods and services in order to buy government bonds—to lend to the government.

Scenario 43: Reducing the Deficit

It may be possible to reduce the deficit by reducing the tax rate. This possibility is suggested by the Laffer curve shown below.

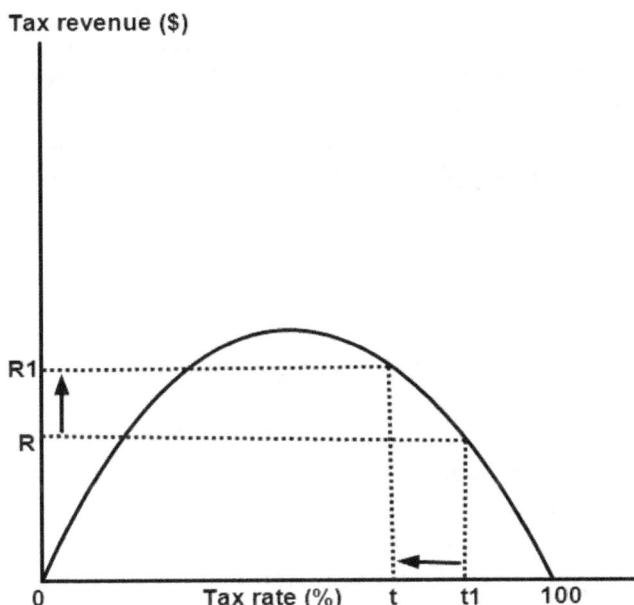

At a tax rate of t1, tax revenue is R. A reduction of the tax rate to t will provide incentives for people to work harder and thus increase the total output of goods and services and income in the economy. This increase in income will produce greater tax revenues for the government (tax revenue increases from R to R1), thus reducing the budget deficit.

Scenario 44: Fiscal Policy and the Budget—Quiz for Feedback

1. **Matching Items**

Column A	Column B
Compulsory payments imposed by a government	B. Taxes
A situation in which government spending equals its revenues	H. Balanced budget
The main source of revenue for the federal government	G. Personal income taxes
A statement of planned revenues and expenditures	E. Budget
Changes in government spending and taxes to achieve desired economic objectives	D. Fiscal policy
A situation in which government spending is less than its revenues	I. Budget surplus
A school of thought that supports active government involvement in the macroeconomy	C. Interventionists
A situation in which government spending is greater than its revenues.	F. Budget deficit

2. **Exercise**

1 d. (At full employment, T = $36 billion, and G = $20 billion, there is therefore a surplus of $16 billion).

2 c. (The budget is balanced when G = T. This occurs at a level of GDP of $50 billion).

3 a. (The full-employment surplus is the difference between revenues (taxes) and government spending. Increasing government spending will reduce that gap).

Scenario 45: Meeting at the Restaurant—Clarification of Budget Deficit

The budget deficit is the amount by which government spending exceeds the amount it collects in taxes. Symbolically, the budget deficit can be expressed as G – T where G is government spending and T is taxes. An increase in the budget deficit means that the government has increased its spending more than it has increased tax receipts. Does this mean an increase in total spending? Not necessarily. One has to consider how the budget deficit is financed. If the budget deficit is financed by borrowing from the private sector—funds which the private sector would otherwise have spent instead of buying government bonds, then the increased budget deficit represents only a shift of purchasing power from the private to the public sector. The increased budget deficit, therefore, does not result in any increase in total spending.

Scenario 46: A Balanced Budget May Not Be All Good

Many people, like you Dad, believe that a balanced budget is always good. That is why so many governments promise to balance their budgets even when they have no intentions of doing so. Maintaining a balanced budget can actually worsen a bad economic situation. Suppose the economy is experiencing a recession. In such a situation, national income and employment are falling. The government's revenues from taxes are declining. This may result in a budget deficit. In order to maintain a balanced budget, the government must reduce its spending. It may also necessitate an increase in tax rates. The result of a reduction in government spending and an increase in tax rates is a reduction in aggregate expenditure. The effect of these actions is illustrated by the following diagram.

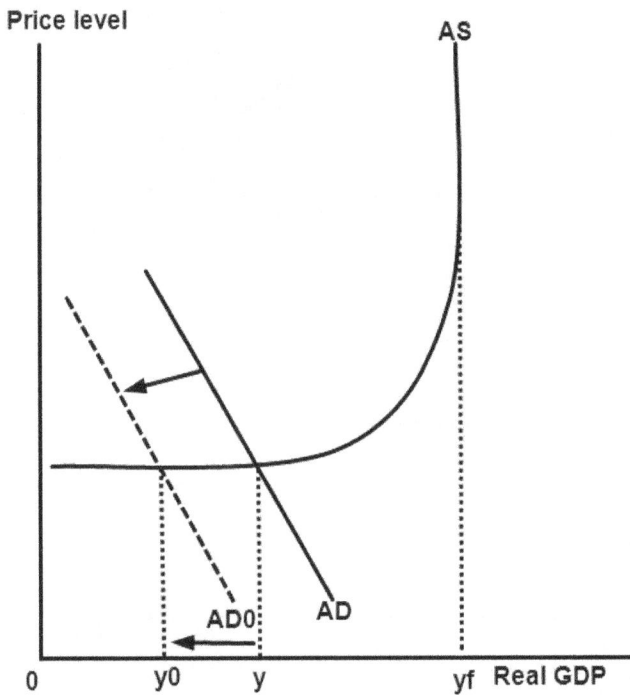

The economy is in equilibrium at a level of real GDP of y, which is significantly below its full-employment output of yf. The economy is experiencing a recession. The reduction in government spending to maintain a balanced budget shifts the AD curve from AD to AD0, and reduces real GDP from y to y0, thus intensifying the recession. Clearly, pursuing a balanced budget in this instance is bad for the economy. It would be better for the government to run the deficit which will have a stimulating effect on the economy.

In an inflationary situation, government tax revenues increase. This may lead to a budgetary surplus. In order to maintain a balanced budget, the government would have to increase its spending and or cut taxes. This action would be expansionary and tend to intensify the inflation. The following diagram illustrates the point. The economy is initially in equilibrium with a price level of P, which is above the non-inflationary level of P0. Maintaining a balanced budget would cause the aggregate demand curve AD to shift from AD to AD1, resulting in the price level rising from P to P1 and worsening the inflationary situation. It can therefore be concluded that a balanced budget intensifies recessionary and inflationary situations.

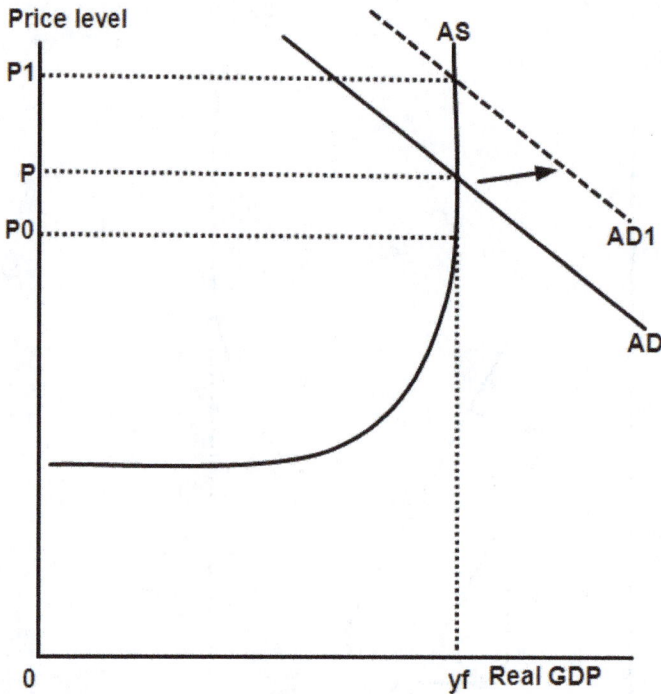

Scenario 47: What Robin Hood Must Have Accomplished. The Effect of Income Redistribution on Total Consumption

Mr. Ambrose's view of the government policy may be taken with a grain of salt; there is at least a grain of truth in it. For one thing, politicians pursue policies that make them popular. After all, they want to win the next election. For another thing, they often do not follow the advice of their economic advisers (see Scenario 5).

Since Mr. Ambrose has a much larger income than Mr. Benjamin does, it follows that Mr. Ambrose's marginal propensity to consume (MPC) is lower than Mr. Benjamin's. Taking $5000, for example, from Mr. Ambrose and giving it to Mr. Benjamin is actually taking money from where it is not likely to reduce personal expenditure on consumer goods and services to any appreciable degree and putting it where it is likely to increase personal consumer spending significantly. The effect is an increase in overall total spending that will stimulate the economy. The activities of Robin Hood who stole from the rich and gave to the poor must have contributed significantly to total spending on consumer goods and services, which must have stimulated the economy.

Scenario 48: Saving at the Movies

O.K. Since you are so eager to hear about saving and the economy, let me explain. Listen carefully. Given the level of income, an increase in saving by consumers like you and me, means that we are reducing our spending on consumer goods and services. Producers may then notice a fall in sales, and consequently reduce production, spending less on the factors of production such as labour and raw materials. Thus, income will fall. If consumers increase their saving and at the same time firms, through borrowing, channel those savings into investment, the economy's capital stock will increase, and the economy's productive capacity will thus increase and that is good for the economy. You are probably thinking that that is not the same thing as getting a discount on movie tickets, and maybe you are right, but you have learnt something tonight. Ha! Ha!

Scenario 49: A Parade of "Marginals". Play the Game

The marginal concepts in macroeconomics include:

Marginal efficiency of capital (MEC): The increase in output resulting from increasing the capital stock by one unit.

Marginal efficiency of investment MEI): The inverse relationship between the rate of interest and the level of investment. This is also referred to as investment demand.

Marginal product of labour (MPL): The extra output produced by employing an additional worker.

Marginal propensity to consume (MPC): The change in consumption resulting from a change in income (MPC = $\Delta C/\Delta Y$ where C is consumption and Y is income). Mathematically, it is the slope of the consumption curve.

Marginal propensity to import (MPM): The change in imports resulting from a change in income (MPM = $\Delta M/\Delta Y$ where M is imports and Y is income).

Marginal propensity to save (MPS): The change in saving resulting from a change in income (MPS = $\Delta S/\Delta Y$ where S is saving and Y is income). Mathematically, it is the slope of the saving curve.

Marginal tax rate (MTR): The fraction of extra income that is paid in taxes (MTR = $\Delta T/\Delta Y$ where T is taxes and Y is income).

Scenario 50: The More You Save, the Less You Save—A Real Paradox

Parsimonia is experiencing what is referred to as the *paradox of thrift* or the *paradox of saving*. The paradox of thrift states that an increase in intended aggregate saving, other things being equal, will lead to a fall in total income and hence to a fall in actual aggregate saving. The paradox of thrift can be defined as the apparent contradiction in the fact that an increase in intended aggregate saving results in a decrease in actual saving. Note that the statement appears to be totally contradictory if the words "intended aggregate" and "actual" are omitted. The statement would then read, "An increase in saving results in a decrease in saving".

There is another dimension to the paradox of thrift. Saving by individuals makes them better off in the future (provided that inflation does not severely reduce the value of their saving) and is therefore considered a virtue. But from an economy-wide perspective, thrift may be considered a societal vice, because it makes the entire economy worse off in the future. In what follows, I illustrate the paradox of thrift graphically.

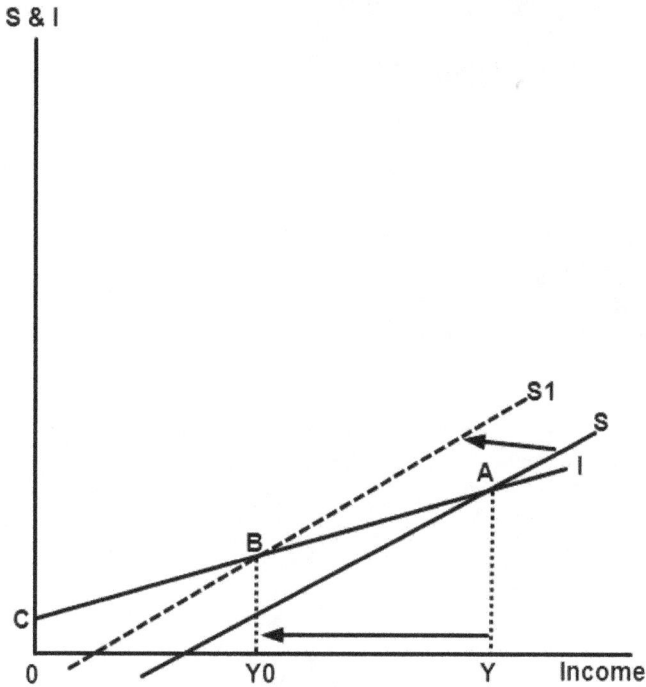

The Investment line I shows that there is autonomous investment of 0C. Thereafter, investment is *induced*, that is, it depends on income. The saving line is upward-sloping indicating that as income increases so does saving.

The saving and investment lines intersect at A at an equilibrium level of income of Y. Saving at this level of income is YA. An increase in saving shifts the saving line up from S to S1. This causes the equilibrium level of income to fall from Y to Y0. The new level of saving is now Y0B, which is less than YA.

Scenario 51: Funny (Not Phony) Math—The Multiplier

The investment multiplier (k) is given by the following formula.

$$k = \frac{1}{1-MPC} \text{ or } \frac{1}{MPS}$$

Since the MPC is given as 0.8, then the investment multiplier can be calculated as:

$$k = \frac{1}{1-0.8} = \frac{1}{0.2} = 5$$

The change in income resulting from an investment spending is given by the formula:

$\Delta Y = k\Delta I$ where Y is income, k is the multiplier, and I is investment.

Therefore, with an investment multiplier of 5, the change in income resulting from an investment of $15 billion is:

$\Delta Y = 5 \times \$15$ billion = **$75 billion.**

Scenario 52: A Moneyless Community Wherein Dwells No Inflation

Inflation is defined as a sustained increase in the general level of prices. A barter economy, as described in the scenario, is one in which goods and services are traded without the use of money. In such an economy, the price of one good or service is expressed in terms of another good or service. Thus, if the price of one good or service, say A, doubles in terms of good B, then it means that the price of good or service B is halved in terms of good A. Hence, in a barter economy, there cannot be any increase in the general level of prices—inflation cannot occur. In that sense then, inflation is a purely monetary phenomenon.

Scenario 53: Notes on Money—The Textbook Cannot Tell All

Notes (Hand-out) on the Desirable Characteristics of Money

Money is defined as anything that is generally accepted as final payment for goods and services, but not anything can serve well as money. Remember the three functions of money: medium of exchange, store of value, and unit of account. The following are the desirable characteristics of money:

General acceptability Whatever serves as money must be generally accepted by the members of the society. If there is reluctance in accepting the item, it will not serve well as a medium of exchange. Even legal tender money will not perform the medium of exchange function if it is not generally accepted as payment for goods and services.

Portability Any item that serves as money must be portable. It must be relatively easy to carry around even large amounts of money because transactions, large and small, are made here, there, and everywhere. A $20 bill is certainly portable, but so is a chequing account. I can write a cheque for $20,000 anywhere.

Durability If money is to serve as a store of value or as a medium of exchange, it must be durable. It must be possible to use it over and over, and if we save it up, it should not go bad like apples or strawberries.

Divisibility If money cannot be divided into smaller denominations, it will not serve as money because it will not be convenient. The divisibility feature of money allows us to make small purchases and to obtain change when a greater sum is offered in payment than the value of the purchase. Books, for example, would not serve well as money because they are not divisible.

Recognisability Another important characteristic of money is that it must be recognizable. Most rational people will be hesitant to accept an item as money if it were not easily recognized. Its role as a medium of exchange will be greatly enhanced if it is easily recognized as money by everyone. Counterfeit money circulates because it so closely resembles the real thing.

Controllability If everyone could manufacture his or her own money, by growing it in his or her backyard, say, then everyone would be well supplied with a stock of money with no one to control the quantity. The value of money would soon fall to zero and it would not function as a medium of exchange.

Scenario 54: Money and Monetary Policy Basics via Pamphlets

Pamphlet A: The Economic Functions of Money

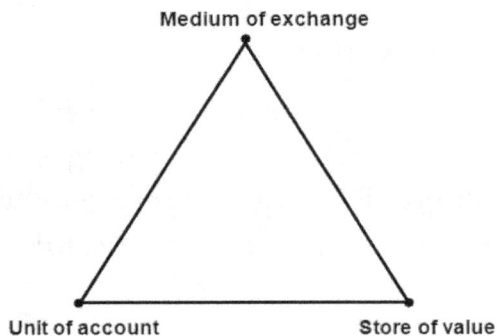

Money is defined as anything that is generally accepted as final payment for goods and services. The items that perform monetary functions in modern societies are notes and coins (currency), and checking accounts at commercial banks. Money performs three fundamental economic functions: (1) It serves as a medium of exchange; (2) it serves as a store of value; and (3) it serves as a unit of account.

Medium of exchange Money serves as a medium of exchange when it is used to pay for goods and services. If I buy a winter jacket for $199.99 and pay for it with cash, cheque, or debit card, I am using money as a medium of exchange. Without money, exchange would have to take place by barter—exchanging goods and services for other goods and services—which is extremely inefficient and time-consuming.

Store of value Money serves as a store of value when members of society hold a portion of their wealth in the form of money. When you earn $500 and you spend $400, keeping $100 in a savings account, you are using money as a store of value or as a liquid asset. Other liquid assets are bonds and stocks, but needless to say, money is the most liquid of all assets.

Unit of account We use money as a common unit for expressing the value of goods and services. For example, let's assume that you are at a shopping mall and you see the price of an item expressed as $59.95. Money is there used to give you information of the monetary value of that item. It is there used as a unit of account or as a measure of value. Without such a single uniform measure of value, it would be indeed difficult to compare prices, wages, and incomes.

Pamphlet B: Monetary Policy against Inflation

What

A

Central Bank

Can Do

Inflation is a continuous rise in the average level of prices. Because it has undesirable consequences for society, it makes good economic sense to control it. Monetary policy—changes in the quantity of money and interest rates by the central bank—can be used to control inflation. Here is how it works. Inflation generally results from attempts by members of society to buy more goods and services than the economy can produce. In order to curb spending and thus slow inflation, the central bank can reduce the quantity of money. As shown in the following graph, when the central bank reduces the quantity of money, from M to M0, the rate of interest rises from r to r1.

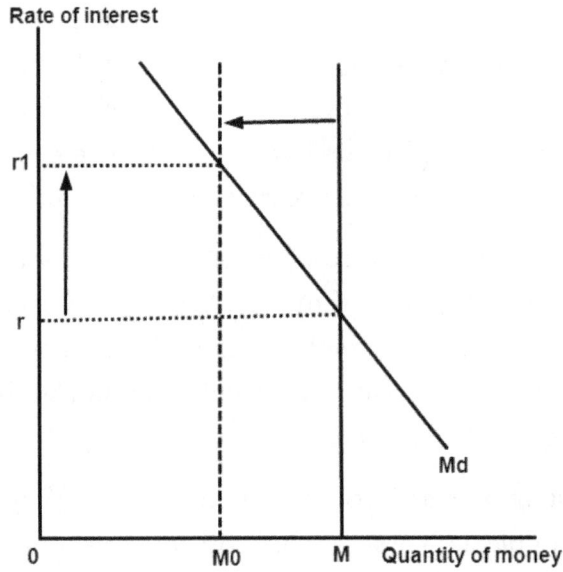

Rate of interest

r1

r

Md

0   M0   M   **Quantity of money**

With the increase in the rate of interest, proposed investment projects that might have been profitable at the lower rate of interest are no longer viable. Also at the higher rate of interest, borrowing for investment purposes is now more costly. For these reasons, the level of investment spending falls. This is illustrated in the following diagram.

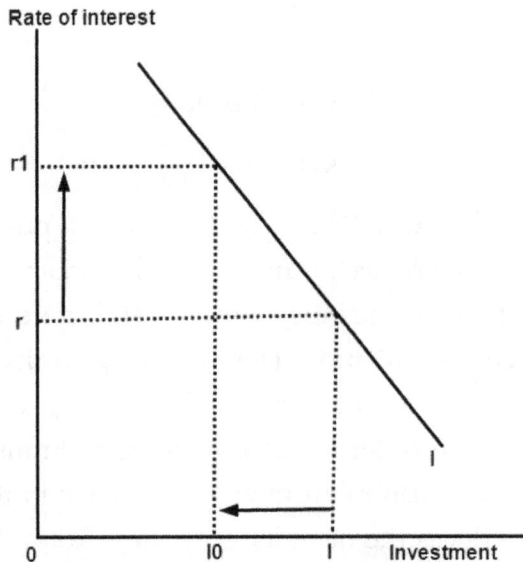

Rate of interest

r1

r

I

0   I0   I   **Investment**

When the rate of interest rises from r to r1, the level of investment spending falls from I to I0. In addition, the level of consumer spending also falls since higher interest rates tend to discourage consumer spending. The effect of the reduction in spending is illustrated in the following diagram.

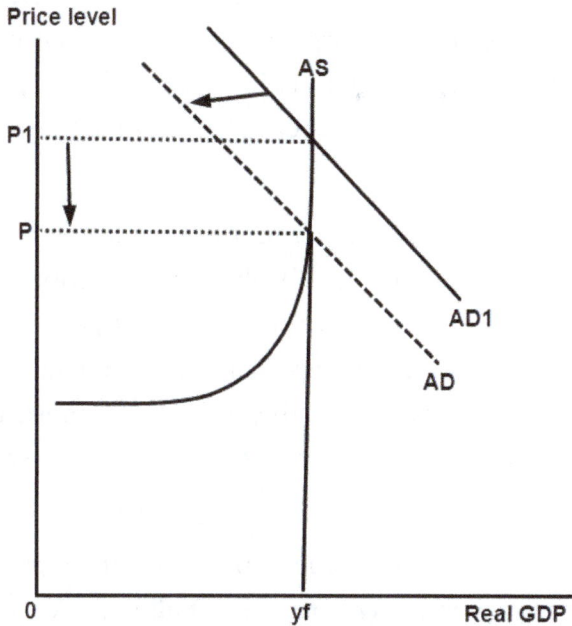

The economy is initially in equilibrium at full employment (yf) with a price level of P1. The desired price level, however, if P, which is just enough to generate the full-employment level of real GDP. The price level P1 is inflationary. The reduction in spending shifts the AD curve from AD1 to AD and reduces the price level from P1 to P. The inflationary pressure is eliminated and a non-inflationary macroeconomic equilibrium is reached.

Pamphlet C: Reasons for Holding Money

Why does anyone hold money? People hold money for three reasons: (1) for transaction purposes, (2) for precautionary purposes, and (3) for speculative purposes.

Transactions demand People hold money in order to pay for the goods and services that they buy. They need money to pay their rent, to pay their mortgages, to purchase groceries, to educate their children, to pay for vacations, etc. The amount of money that they will hold for this purpose depends on their income. The higher the level of income, the more transactions people are likely to make; hence they would want to hold more money. In this case, the money they hold is to function as a medium of exchange.

Precautionary demand There are uncertainties in life. People will hold some money to meet unforeseen contingencies such as a broken air condition system, a damaged car engine, sudden illness, etc. In times of uncertainty, a greater amount of money is held for precautionary purposes. The precautionary demand for money depends on the level of income. In this case, as in the case of the transactions demand, the money people hold is intended to function as a medium of exchange, should the need arise.

The speculative demand People hold money for speculative purposes. When the purchasing power of money is rising (prices are falling), people will tend to hold more money. By so doing, they hope to gain by purchasing goods at lower prices in the future. The higher the rate of interest, the smaller the quantity of money that people will hold for this purpose. Instead of holding money, they will tend to hold interest-earning assets such as bonds. The lower the rate of interest, the greater the amount of money that people will want to hold.

Scenario 55: At Least One Member of the Board is Confused about Banking

The error that the board member has made is rather typical. It is a common misconception about the deposit expansion process. Although it is possible for a bank to lend out its excess reserves, it is not in its best interest to do so. If the bank behaved in that manner it will fail to earn maximum returns on its loans. Instead, the bank grants a loan by creating a deposit for the borrower and keeping the excess reserves to meet its desired reserve requirement. By behaving in this manner, the bank can extend a great deal more loans on which it can earn interest income. Although it may seem so, the bank does not really lend out its excess reserves, but it does lend out an amount equivalent to its excess reserves.

The point is illustrated in the following table.

Steps	Deposits ($)	Reserve requirements ($)	Loans = excess reserves ($)
1	1,000.00	100.00	900.00
2	900.00	90.00	810.00
3	810.00	81.00	729.00
4	729.00	72.90	656.10
5	656.10	65.61	590.49
6	590.49	59.05	531.44

In step 1, a customer deposits $1,000 cash in her chequing account at a bank. If the desired cash reserve is 10% of deposits, the bank keeps $100 and has excess reserves of $900. In step 2, another customer borrows $900. The bank grants the loan by crediting $900 to the borrower's account. Note that the bank does not give the borrower its excess reserves of $900. Instead, it has created a new deposit by granting the loan. The new deposit of $900, however, is an amount equal to the bank's excess reserves. The process continues with step 3 where a customer borrows $810. Again, the bank grants the loan by crediting the borrower's account with $810. If the bank had lent out its excess reserves, it would not be able to make the loan because it would not be able to satisfy its reserve requirement. The process continues with further steps until all the excess reserves end up as desired reserves.

Scenario 56: Monetary Policy to Combat Inflation and Recession—A Two-edged Sword?

The AD/AS model is appropriate for explaining how monetary policy can be used to combat an inflationary situation. In the following diagram, the economy is in macro-equilibrium with a price level of P and a real GDP of Y.

However, this equilibrium is above the full-employment level of real GDP. In other words, the economy is experiencing an inflationary gap. The price level needs to be reduced. As can be seen from the graph, if it were possible to shift the aggregate demand (AD) curve from its original position to AD0, the price level would fall from P to P0, and macro-equilibrium would be achieved at the full-employment level of Yf.

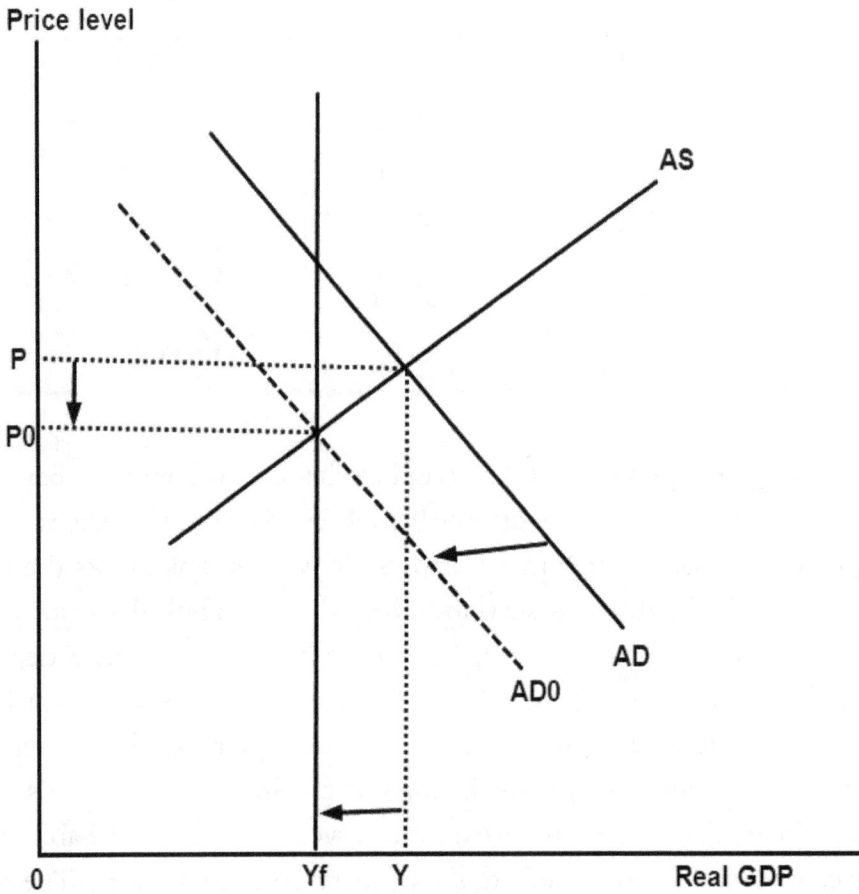

Price level

AS

AD

AD0

P

P0

0   Yf   Y   **Real GDP**

To achieve this, the central bank can reduce the money supply. Other things being equal, the rate of interest will rise and private-sector spending on consumption and investment) will fall, resulting in a reduction in total spending which will shift the AD curve to the left from AD to AD0 as shown in the diagram. The price level falls from P to P0, and real GDP moves to its full-employment level of Yf. The inflationary pressure has been eliminated.

To deal with the recession in the forecast, the central bank can plan an expansionary monetary policy to be implemented at the opportune time. The following diagram can be used to illustrate how the central bank can use monetary policy to combat a recessionary situation.

Price level

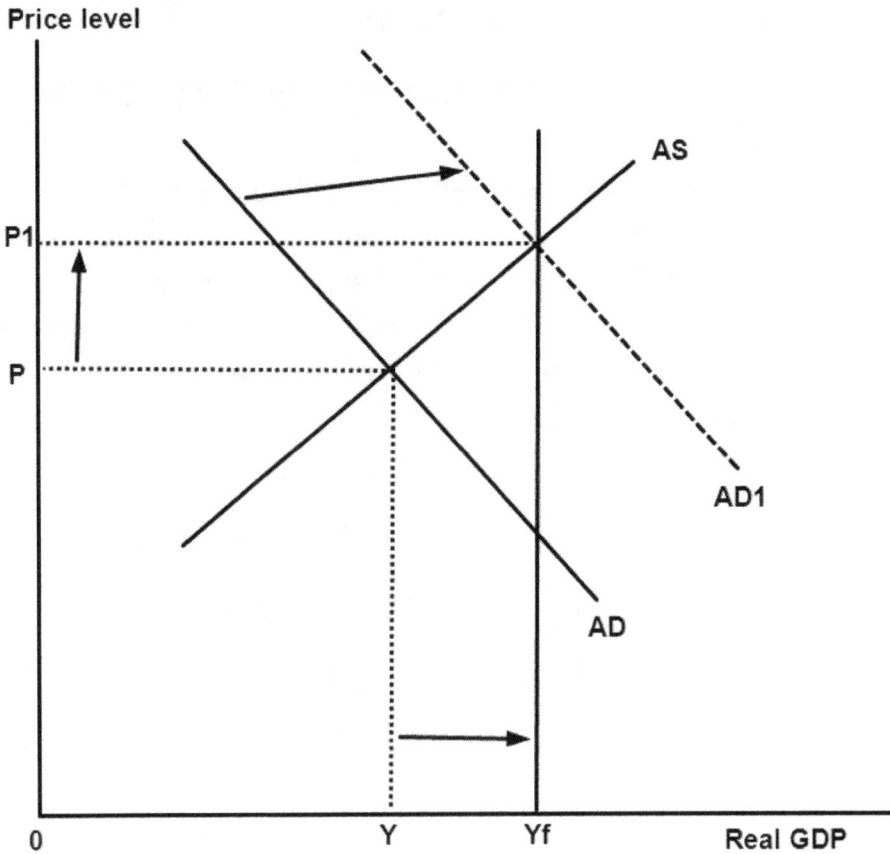

Initially, the economy is in equilibrium with a price level of P and a real GDP of Y. This equilibrium is below the potential real GDP of Yf, so a recessionary gap exists. What is required is a policy that will shift the aggregate demand (AD) curve from AD to AD1 as shown in the diagram. The central bank can increase the money supply. This will lower interest rates and cause consumption and investment to increase. The increase in consumption and investment will shift the AD curve to the right to AD1. The economy is now in equilibrium at full employment with a price level of P1. The recessionary gap is eliminated.

Scenario 57: Tell It with Graphs: Money Matters

a) **Effect of an increase in the money supply when the economy is in the Keynesian Range.**

In the following diagram, the economy is initially in equilibrium in the Keynesian range with a real GDP of Y and a price level of P. If the central bank increases the money supply, interest rates will fall, and this will stimulate consumption and investment, shifting the aggregate demand curve from AD to AD1 as shown in the diagram. As a consequence, the equilibrium level of real GDP rises from Y to Y1, while the price level remains unchanged at P.

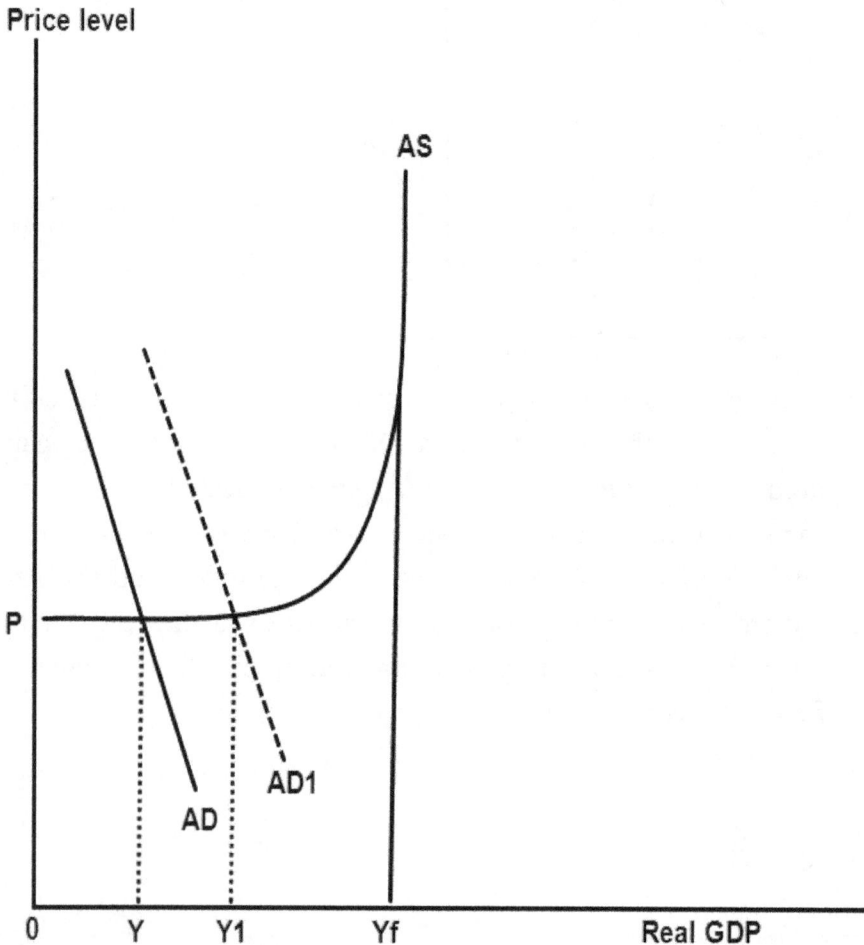

b) **Effects of a decrease in the money supply when the economy is operating in the classical range.**

The economy is in equilibrium in the classical range at a price level of P and a real GDP of Yf as shown in the following diagram.

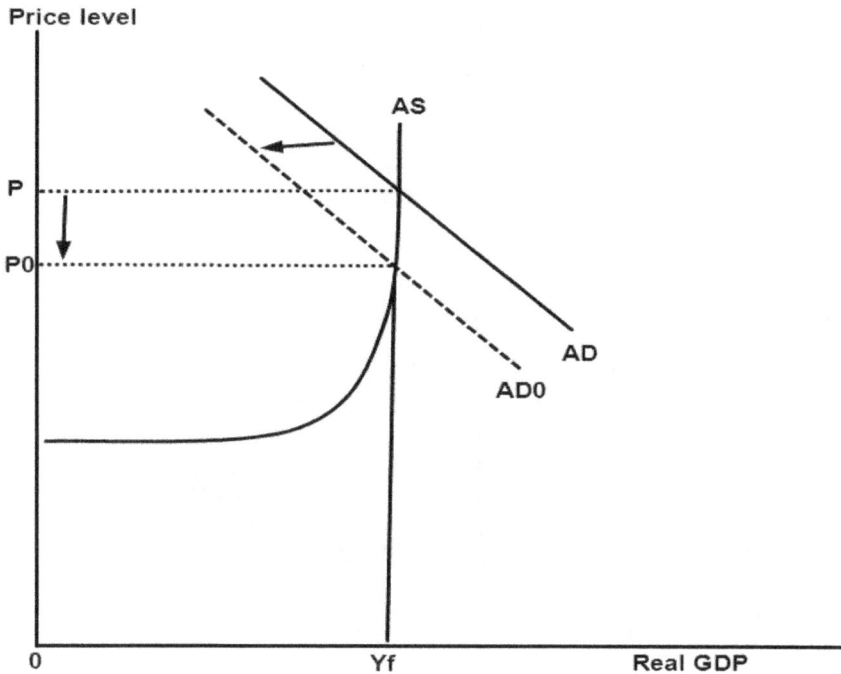

If the central bank reduces the money supply, interest rates will rise and private-sector (consumption and investment) spending will fall. This fall in spending will shift the aggregate demand curve from AD to AD0, causing the price level to fall. Real GDP, however, will remain at its potential Yf.

c) **The effect of a reduction in interest rates when the economy is in the intermediate range.**

As the following diagram shows, the initial equilibrium position is a price level of P and a real GDP of Y. A reduction in interest rates will stimulate consumer spending and investment spending, which will shift the aggregate demand curve from AD to AD1 as shown. This increase in aggregate demand results in an increase in the equilibrium price level from P to P1, and an increase in equilibrium real GDP from Y to Y1.

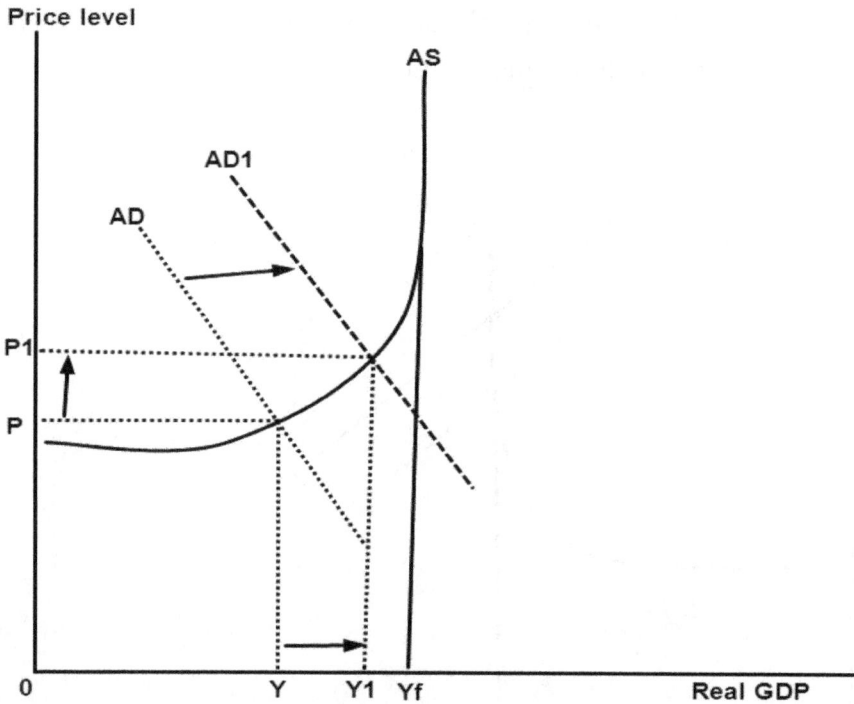

d) Effects of a tight monetary policy when the economy is operating in the Keynesian range.

As illustrated in the following graph, the economy is in equilibrium with a price level of P and a real GDP of Y. A tight monetary policy is a reduction in the money supply and an increase in interest rates. Such a policy will reduce both consumption and investment, leading to a shift of the aggregate demand curve from AD to AD0. The effect of this reduction in aggregate demand is to reduce the equilibrium level of real GDP from Y to Y0, while leaving the equilibrium price level at P.

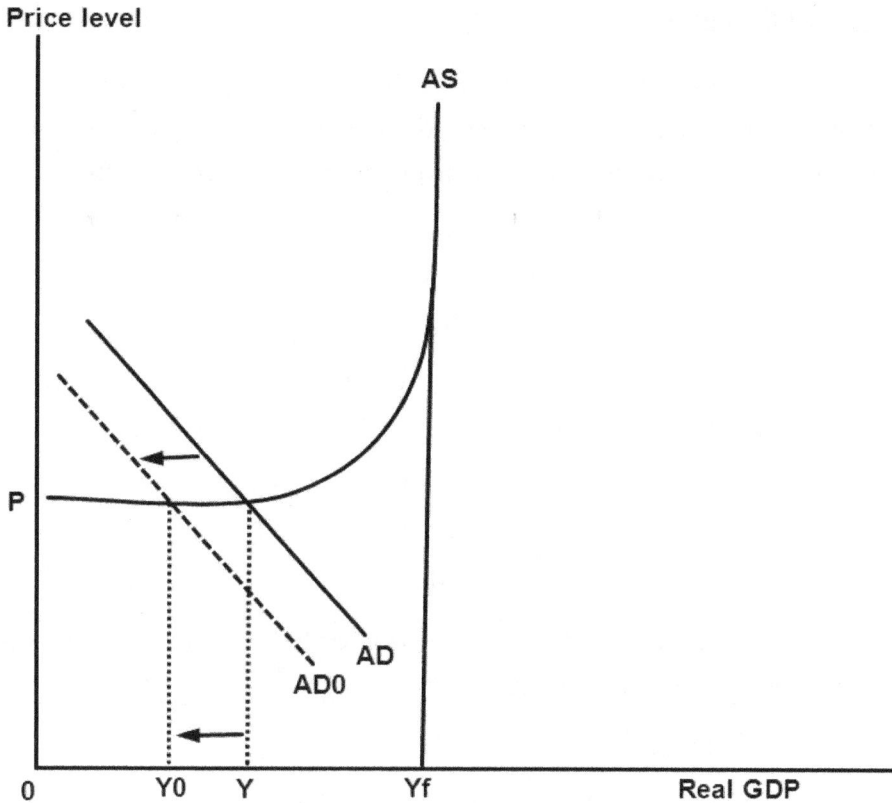

Scenario 58: Presentation at the Money Convention

The quantity theory of money refers to the proposition that a change in the quantity of money (i.e., the money stock) causes a proportional change in the average level of prices. This theory owes its origin to Jean Bodin (1530-1596), who, in his *Answers to the Paradoxes of Mr. Malestroit* (1566), singled out money as the main reason for increases in prices. In fact, there are many versions of this theory, but at the moment, I will focus on what is referred to as the *crude quantity theory* developed by Irving Fisher (1867-1947).

Two concepts are necessary for a clear understand of this *classical* version of the theory. These concepts are the velocity of circulation of money and the equation of exchange. Let us first look at the velocity of circulation.

The Velocity of Circulation

The velocity of circulation of money refers to the number of times, on average, that a unit of money (such as a dollar or a pound) is spent per year in purchasing final goods and services. The velocity of circulation can be expressed symbolically as:

$$V = \frac{P \times T}{M}$$

where V is the velocity of circulation, P is the price level, M is the quantity of money, and T is the volume of transactions. Of course, P × T is GDP, thus

$$V = \frac{GDP}{M}$$

We turn now to the other concept that we need in order to understand the quantity theory, that is, the equation of exchange.

The Equation of Exchange

The equation of exchange may be expressed as the following identity:

MV = PT

where the symbols M, V, P, and T have exactly the same meanings as in the velocity equation referred to earlier.

Let us examine the equation of exchange a little more closely. The left-hand side of the equation (MV) is simply the amount spent in purchasing goods and services. The right-hand side of the equation (PT) is the total value of all transactions. Since the total amount spent in purchasing all goods and services must equal the value of the goods and services, the equation of exchange is true by definition. MV and PT are just different ways of looking at the same thing. Note that up to this point, we do not have a theory. The equation of exchange is just a tautology.

The Quantity Theory

The neoclassical economists made certain assumptions about the variables in the equation of exchange which enabled them to arrive at a theory of money and the price level. Specifically, they assumed:

1. The quantity of money is determined by the monetary authorities. Hence M is given.
2. The velocity of circulation, V, is determined by institutional factors such as payments habits, and the frequency of receipt of income, and is therefore independent of M, P, and T. This makes V a constant.
3. The volume of transactions, T, would remain fixed at the full-employment level, at least in the short run.

Thus, P, the average level of prices, is the only passive variable in the equation of exchange. What this means is that the price level does not affect the other variables, but it may be affected by them. The effect of these assumptions can be seen readily if we divide the equation of exchange by V to obtain

$$M = \frac{T}{V} \times P$$

With T/V being constant, M is directly proportional to P. The conclusion to be drawn from this discussion is that the price level is determined by the quantity of money. Changes in the quantity of money cause proportional changes in the price level.

Scenario 59: Quantitative Easing! Is this a New Concept or Is It Just a New Name for an Old Concept?

Open market operations (OMO) is a tried and tested instrument of monetary policy. It refers to the buying and selling of government securities by a central bank on the open market. If the central bank wants to pursue an expansionary monetary policy by increasing the quantity of money, it can do so by purchasing securities on the open market.

Quantitative easing (QE) is an expansionary monetary policy tool whereby the central bank buys extremely large quantities of various types of securities in an attempt to increase liquidity and thus increase investment and stimulate economic activity. This tool is used when interest rates approach zero and traditional expansionary monetary policy fails to stimulate economic activity.

The idea of QE may be better understood by comparing it with open market operations (OMO). QE is essentially an expansion of OMO, but there are notable differences. First, QE occurs on a much larger scale than OMO, and involves a much larger variety of assets. OMO involves purchasing short-term government securities while QE involves purchasing long-term securities, even mortgages. Thus, OMO affect short-term interest rates while QE affects long-term interest rates.

Scenario 60: Newspaper Reports Policy Makers' Talk. Fiscal policy vs Monetary Policy

Fiscal policy refers to changes in government spending and taxes in order to achieve desired economic conditions. Fiscal policy variables are therefore government expenditure and taxes levied on individuals and businesses. Increases in the levels of govern expenditure and reductions in taxes will tend to increase GDP and employment. Such a policy is referred to as an expansionary fiscal policy. The following Keynesian cross diagram illustrates an expansionary fiscal policy.

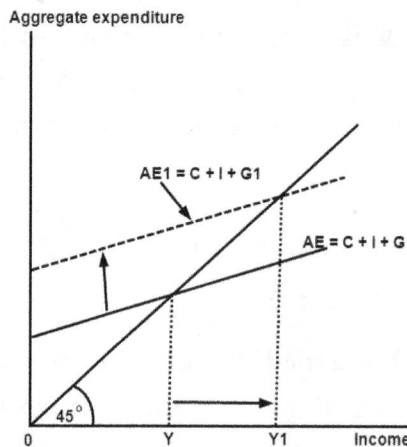

It is assumed that the economy is closed. The product market is initially in equilibrium at Y. An increase in government expenditure from G to G1 will shift the aggregate expenditure (AE) line from AE to AE1, resulting in an increase in income (and employment) from Y to Y1. A tax cut will have the same effect.

Reductions in the levels of government expenditure and increases in taxes will tend to reduce inflation. Such a policy is referred to as a contractionary fiscal policy. The following diagram will help to illustrate a contractionary fiscal policy.

Aggregate expenditure

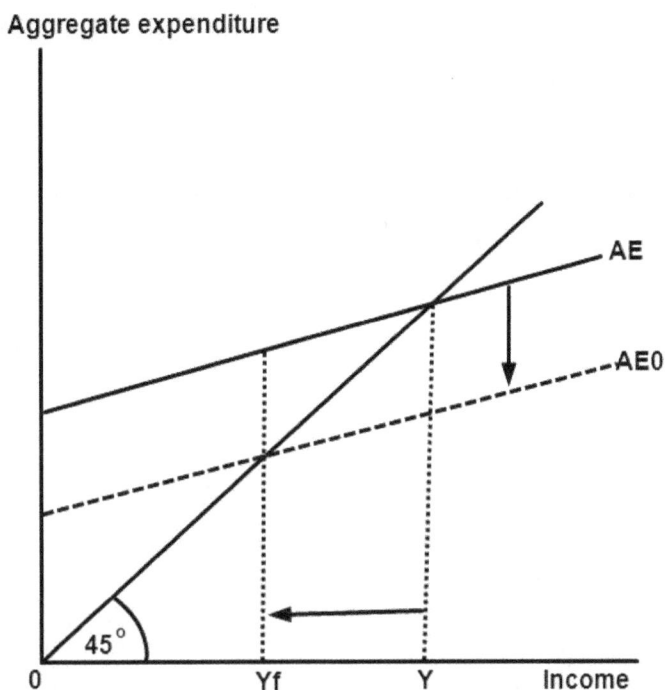

The initial equilibrium level of income is Y, but this level is above the full-employment level of Yf. The economy is experiencing inflation because of spending above the full-employment level of output. To reduce the amount of spending, the government can reduce its own level of expenditure and raise taxes. This policy will lower the AE curve from AE to AE0 and rid the economy of the inflationary pressure.

Monetary policy refers to changes in the quantity of money and or interest rates by the monetary authorities. Monetary policy variables are therefore the money stock and interest rates. Increases in the quantity of money (money stock) and reductions in interest rates are expansionary and will tend to stimulate economic activity. Such a policy is an expansionary or easy monetary policy. The process by which an expansionary monetary policy affects income and employment is as follows:

$$\Delta Ms\uparrow \rightarrow r\downarrow \rightarrow (C \& I)\uparrow \rightarrow AE\uparrow$$

where Ms represents the money supply, r is the rate of interest, C is consumer spending, I is investment, and AE is aggregate expenditure. This economic stimulus will increase income and employment.

To combat an inflationary situation, the monetary authorities can reduce the money supply and raise interest rates. Such a policy is a contractionary or tight monetary policy. The process by which a contractionary monetary policy affects income and the price level is as follows:

$$\Delta Ms\downarrow \rightarrow r\uparrow \rightarrow (C \ \& \ I)\downarrow \rightarrow AE\downarrow$$

where the symbols have the same meanings as before. This policy will reduce income and lower the price level.

Scenario 61: Internet Blames Hike in Oil Price for Inflation in the 1970s

This is a classic example of what is called the *post hoc ergo propter hoc* fallacy. "Post hoc ergo propter hoc", also called the *sequential fallacy*, is a Latin expression meaning "after this, therefore because of this." The fallacy lies in the argument that because one event follows another event, it is caused by that other event—an argument that is not necessarily valid. In this case, the inflation of the 1970s has been attributed to the increase in the price of oil because it followed the increase in the price of OPEC oil. It is quite possible, however, that the inflation could have been caused by other factors.

The fact is, economists are in general agreement that an increase in cost (such as an increase in the price of an important input such as oil) will be inflationary only if it is accompanied by an increase in the money supply. Consider the inflation of the 1970s referenced in the scenario. This is often cited as a classic example of *cost-push inflation*. OPEC raised the price of its oil by 70% in 1973. Consequently, the prices of petroleum-related products increased. If these price increases were offset by price reductions in other sectors of the economy, there would have been no increase in the average level of prices. Why were there no offsetting price reductions elsewhere in the economy? After all, given a certain amount of money, if we spend more on oil and products made from petroleum, then we have a smaller amount to spend on other things. Only if the monetary authorities *validate* the cost-push inflation, that is, increase the money supply, will there be overall increases in the price level. The inflation then is due to increases in the money supply and not to an increase in the price of oil. Just because it's on the Internet does not make it true.

Scenario 62: Stagflation. Oops! How Can This Be? Look to the Other Side

The following AD/AS diagram will help to illustrate the possibility of stagflation in an economy.

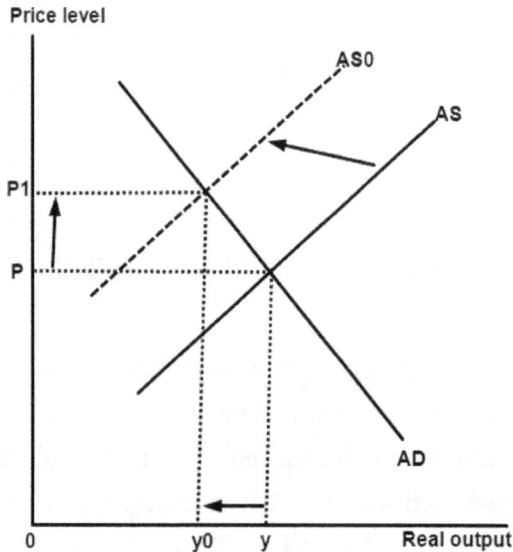

AD and AS are the initial aggregate demand and aggregate supply curves. The initial equilibrium level of real output is y, and the price level is P. If the aggregate supply curve shifts from AS to AS0, the real level of output falls from y to y0, and the price level increases from P to P1. Clearly, demand-side shifts increase the price level and real output and employment or reduce the price level and real GDP and employment. We must turn to the supply-side for an explanation of stagflation. This analysis points clearly to supply shifts as a cause of rising prices accompanied by falling employment and output, that is, stagflation.

Scenario 63: Return to DeFicitia—A Matter of Stagflation

It is obvious that demand-side policies will not work to solve the problem of stagflation. An expansionary demand-side policy will reduce the rate of unemployment but will raise the price level. A contractionary demand-side policy will reduce the rate of inflation but will worsen the unemployment problem. Solving the problem of stagflation using demand-side policies seems to be a conundrum. Let us look at the supply side.

Shifting the aggregate supply (AS) curve to the right, other things being equal, will increase output and employment and lower the price level at the same time. The following diagram illustrates.

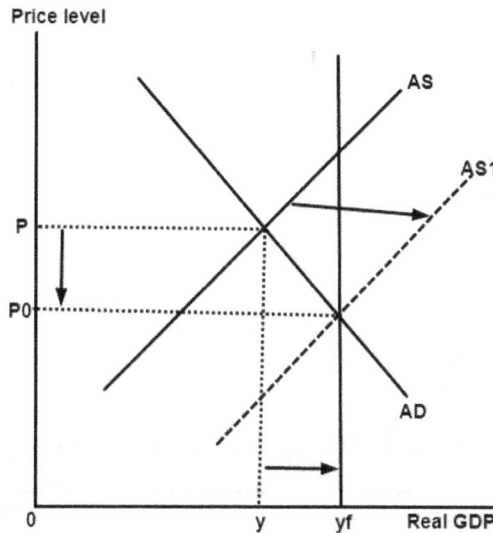

Suppose that the economy is initially in equilibrium with a price level of P and a real GDP of y. Suppose also that this price level is considered to be inflationary and that y represents output with substantial unemployment. Shifting the AS curve from AS to AS1 lowers the price level from P to P0, and increases output (and employment) from y to yf. This solves the stagflation problem. To shift the AS curve to the right, the Government of DeFicitia can improve its human capital through training, encourage technological improvement, and give incentives such as tax cuts for firms to increase their capital.

Scenario 64: What Kind of Trap You Say? When Monetary Policy Fails

The situation described by the economist is referred to as the *liquidity trap*. It is argued that a situation is possible in which increases in the money supply have no effect in reducing the rate of interest. In such a situation, the liquidity preference (demand for money) curve is flat when it intersects the money supply curve. The situation is illustrated in the following diagram.

Rate of interest

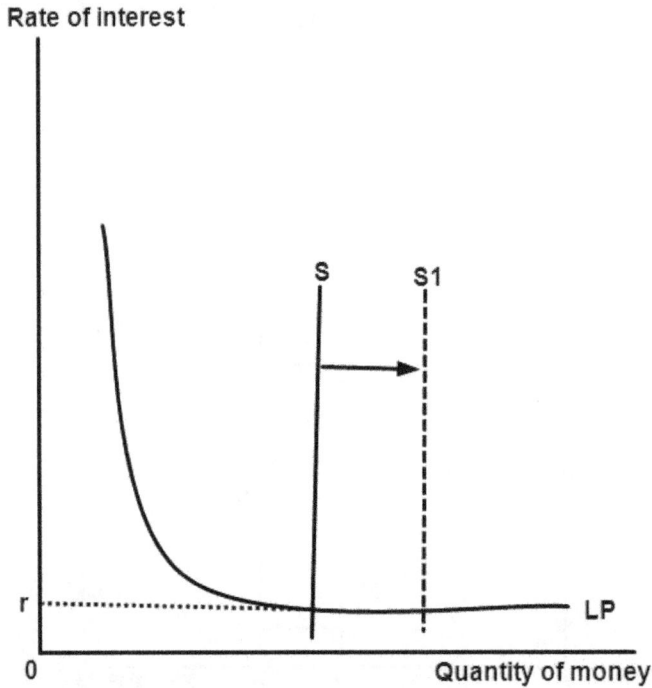

The initial equilibrium rate of interest r, is determined by the intersection of the liquidity preference (LP) curve, and the money supply curve S. An increase in the money supply from S to S1 has no effect on the rate of interest. This situation occurs when the rate of interest is so low that individuals and businesses prefer to hold exceptionally large amounts of money over other forms of assets.

If the economy is in a liquidity trap, some economists, including the one in this scenario, believe that expansionary monetary policy will be ineffective as a means of stimulating economic activity. In the past when interest rates have been relatively high for an extended period of time, not much attention was paid to the liquidity trap and it was largely considered to be of theoretical interest only. However, in recent years, countries such as Switzerland, Sweden, Israel, Japan, and Germany, among others, have experienced interest rates hovering around 0%, and this has revived interest in the concept of the liquidity trap.

Scenario 65: A Class Project—Rational Expectations

Introduction

The idea of rational expectations was developed by an economics professor by the name of John Muth in the 1960s. The theory of rational expectations assumes that decision-makers understand the factors involved in inflation and that they use the relevant information in forming their expectations about inflation. The rational expectations theory therefore predicts that, on average, people's inflationary expectations and their consequent wage and price decisions will be correct.

Proponents of the Rational Expectations Hypothesis

Proponents of the rational expectation hypothesis include prominent economists such as Robert Lucas, Thomas Sargent, and Neil Wallace. According to these economists, people's expectations, and hence their decisions, are based on government policies, the effects of which are known in advance. Rational expectations theorists contend that markets are efficient and that firms use all the available information to make decisions that will accomplish their objectives of profit maximization. Unemployment above the natural rate, that is, the rate consistent with price stability, according to rational expectations theorists, is voluntary because workers know that they can find employment by accepting lower wages.

Critics of the Rational Expectations Hypothesis

Critics of the rational expectations theory claim that the theory is not so rational. They claim that the inflationary process is extremely complex and that it is unreasonable to assume that people in general understand the factors that determine inflation. It is also unreasonable, claim the critics, to expect people to know precisely the effects of government policies. One economist, Franco Modigliani in particular, was critical of the rational expectations hypothesis, claiming that it was inconsistent with the evidence. The rational expectation hypothesis leads to the conclusion that unemployment should deviate only slightly from the natural rate, but, according to Modigliani, actual events refuted this conclusion.

The rational expectations hypothesis has implications for economic stabilization policy. Suppose policymakers use monetary policy and fiscal policy to reduce unemployment. According to the rational expectations hypothesis, people will know the effect of these policies on the rate of inflation. They will expect the rate of inflation to increase and they will expect interest rates to rise as well. Accordingly, workers will demand wage increases in order to protect their real wage. With expectations of higher interest rates and higher wages, firms would not find it profitable to undertake new investment projects. Expansionary monetary and fiscal policies will thus be frustrated. Monetary and fiscal policies, then, will be successful only if they come as complete surprises to decision-makers.

Conclusion

The rational expectations hypothesis is a useful device for modeling decision-making, and it has become an important technique in economics. In macroeconomics, it suggests that policymakers should consider how macroeconomic stabilization policies are implemented since such policies may have little or no effect in achieving economic stability.

Scenario 66: Inflation Tax. Is This a Myth or Is It Political Economy?

An inflation tax seems to be a strange concept. One hears about income tax, property tax, education levy or school tax, water tax, sales tax, etc. One also hears of taxes on the profits of businesses. There is even a welcome tax in some jurisdictions when you buy a house and move into the community. When you pay a tax, you actually use money to do so, and you usually receive some kind of receipt to certify that the tax has been paid. This is not the case with an inflation tax. What exactly then, is an inflation tax? First, I thought that an inflation tax was just the extra tax that the government collects on increases in nominal income that is due to inflation. But that would be an income tax nonetheless.

Upon diligent research, I found out what the inflation tax really is. The government spends a great deal of money on the military and defence, social programs, education, health, the environment, interest on the public debt, etc. Some of this expenditure is covered by taxes on individuals and businesses. However governments often resort to the printing press and print money to pay for some of these services. When the government continually prints a great deal of money and spends it, inflation is a likely outcome. All those who hold money find that their money loses purchasing power. The government gets the money to spend but those who hold money have lost some command over the amount of goods and services that they can buy. That is the inflation tax. The result is the same as a tax that reduces the amount of goods and services that taxpayers can buy. The difference is that other taxes are visible while the inflation tax is invisible, but it is no less real.

Scenario 67: Currency Tied to Oil?

The external value of the Oilando currency is determined by demand and supply. When the price of oil rises, it will have little or no impact on the quantity of Oilando oil demanded by Undercan. Undercan will therefore require more Oilando dollars to pay for oil. This increase in demand for Oilando dollars, other things being equal, will increase the value of the Oilando dollar in terms of Undercan dollars. This explains the close relationship between the price of oil and the value of the Oilando currency.

Scenario 68: A Pamphlet on the Central Bank and Foreign Exchange

THE CENTRAL BANK
AND
FOREIGN EXCHANGE

For countries on a fixed exchange rate system, how does the rate stay fixed once it is established? If a country is on a flexible exchange rate system, an increase in demand for its exports will increase the demand for its currency and its exchange rate will rise. But what if the country is on a fixed exchange rate system? An increase in the demand for its exports will result in an increase in demand for its currency, but the value of its currency is not allowed to rise. What happens in this case is that the central bank enters the foreign exchange market and sells the country's currency (buys foreign currencies) on the foreign exchange market, and thus maintains the established value of the fixed currency. The central bank pursues the opposite course if there is a fall in the demand for its currency. The following diagram illustrates the process whereby the fixed currency is maintained. We assume that Rigidia (a fictitious country) is on a fixed exchange rate regime.

Price of Rigidia $

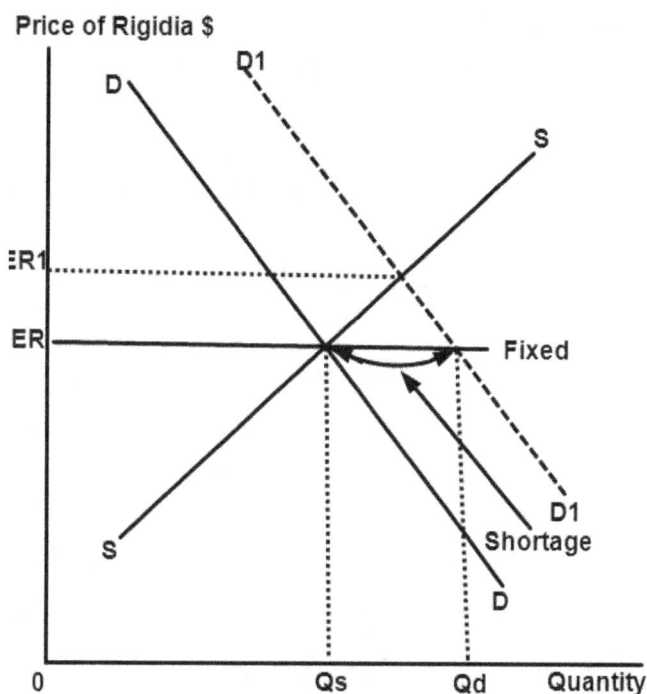

The value of Rigidia's dollar is assumed to be fixed at ER in the diagram. If the demand for exports increases the demand for Rigidian dollars from DD to D1D1, the market would have forced a flexible exchange rate up to ER1, but the fixed rate would remain at ER, causing a shortage to exist. The central bank would then intervene in the foreign exchange market and supply the shortage (Qd – Qs) so that the exchange rate remains at the fixed rate of ER. For a fall in the demand for Rigidian dollars, the central bank would enter the foreign exchange market and buy Rigidian dollars in order to prop up its value. Thus, the continuous intervention of the central bank maintains the fixed exchange rate.

Scenario 69: How Much Does It Cost? Can I Afford It? It's British. That Depends on the Exchange Rate

1. The price of the car is £35,000. With the exchange rate being £1 = $1.95, the price of the car in dollars would be:

$$35,000 \times 1.95 = \$68,250$$

Since David wants to spend no more than $65,000 for the car, he cannot afford to buy it.

2. In order for him to be able to afford the car, £35,000 would have to be equal to $65,000. This means that £1 would have to be equal to:

$$65,000 \div 35,000 = \$1.86$$

The exchange rate would have to fall from £1 = $1.95 to £1 = $1.86

Scenario 70: To Flex or Not to Flex: Advantages and Disadvantages of Flexible Exchange Rates

A flexible exchange rate system is one in which the exchange rate is determined by the market forces of demand and supply. This exchange rate regime has advantages and disadvantages as indicated in the following table.

Advantages and Disadvantages of a Flexible Exchange Rate System

Advantages	Disadvantages
No direct intervention is necessary to achieve equilibrium in the foreign exchange market. The exchange rate adjusts automatically to changes in demand and supply and thus maintains equilibrium. There is therefore no need to maintain foreign reserves in order to peg the exchange rate. A flexible exchange rate frees monetary policy so that it can be used to stabilize the economy. A flexible exchange rate system helps to insulate a country against foreign inflationary pressures. Suppose there is inflation in country B while country A is experiencing relative price stability. Exports from country A to country B will increase as residents of country B switch to relatively cheaper goods from country A. At the same time, imports into country A from country B will fall as residents of country A reduce the quantity of relatively expensive goods demanded from country B. The resulting increase in demand for goods from country A will tend to increase prices in country A. The exchange rate will rise and thus prevent prices in country A from rising. The inflation in country B does not spill over into country A.	The uncertainty associated with flexible exchange rates discourages the flow of international trade. It is important for international traders to know what they will pay for their imports of goods and services that they will receive for their exports of goods and services. Trade cannot be expected to flourish in an environment of uncertainty and insecurity. Flexible exchange rates may affect a country adversely. For example, an appreciation of the value of country A's currency means that foreign goods become relatively less expensive to residents of country A. Lower-priced imports will then compete with goods produced in country A, and consumers may purchase foreign goods instead of goods produced in country A. This, in turn, may lead to reductions in income and increases in unemployment in country A.

Scenario 71: To Peg or Not to Peg: Advantages and Disadvantages of Fixed Exchange Rates

Advantages and Disadvantages of Fixed Exchange Rates

Advantages	Disadvantages
A fixed exchange rate provides certainty. International traders can arrange their transactions with confidence knowing that prices and costs will not change in the interim. A fixed exchange rate, because of its stability, encourages investment. Other things being equal, a stable environment is more desirable for investors than an unstable one.	Maintaining a fixed exchange rate may force a country to adopt a monetary policy with undesirable domestic effects in order to be able to maintain the exchange rate at its fixed level. For example, a restrictive monetary policy with high interest rates may be necessary to maintain the official level of the exchange rate. Such a policy, however, may result in high unemployment and low economic growth. A fixed exchange rate may cause an imbalance in the country's current account. For example, if the country's currency is overvalued at its currently fixed level, a current account deficit could develop.

PART VI SOMEWHAT INTEGRATIVE

Scenario 72: Monetary Policy to Stimulate Economic Activity. Putting It Together

A recession exists when the economy is operating at a level of real output and employment that is significantly below the full-employment level or the potential level of real GDP. The existence of such a situation is undesirable because it represents a loss of real output of goods and services to society. Monetary policy, defined as changes in the money supply and interest rates by the central bank, can be used to tackle a recession. A recession generally results from a deficiency in total spending. In such a case, total spending is not enough to purchase all the goods and services produced by the economy. Inventories of finished goods pile up, and firms reduce their production levels, laying off workers in the process. An increase in unemployment is one of the negative consequences of a recession. In order to encourage the members of society to increase their spending and thus stimulate economic activity, the central bank can increase the money supply. As shown in the following graph, the initial market equilibrium rate of interest is r where the demand for money curve and the money supply cure intersect. If the central bank increases the money supply from Ms to Ms1, the rate of interest falls from r to r0.

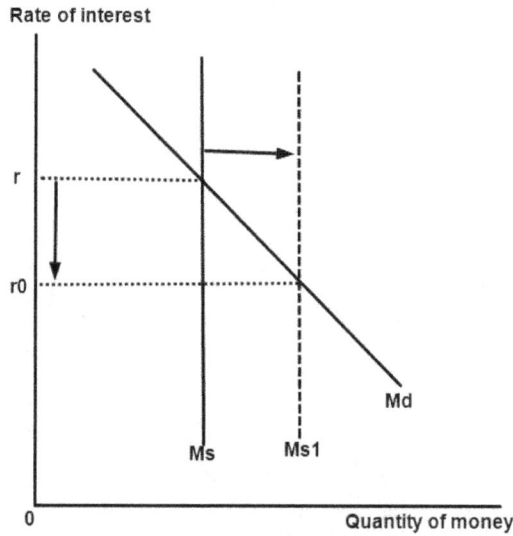

Rate of interest

r

r0

Md

Ms   Ms1

0   Quantity of money

When the rate of interest falls, proposed investment projects that might not have been profitable at the higher rate of interest have now become viable at the lower rate. Also at the lower rate of interest, borrowing for investment purposes is now less costly. For these reasons, the level of investment spending will rise. This is illustrated in the following diagram.

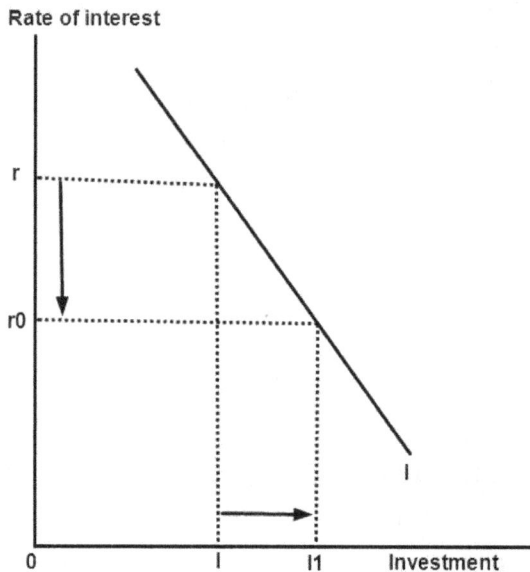

Rate of interest

r

r0

I

0   I   I1   Investment

Initially, the rate of interest is r and the level of investment is I. When the rate of interest falls from r to r0, the level of investment spending rises from I to I1. In addition, the level of consumer spending also rises since lower interest rates tend to encourage consumer spending. The effect of the increase in spending is illustrated in the following diagram.

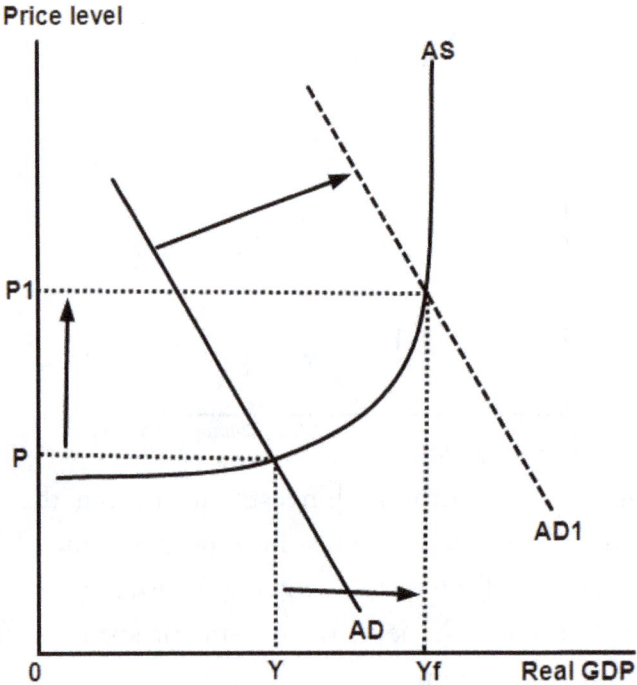

The economy is initially in equilibrium at Y, with a price level of P. The desired level of real GDP is Yf which is the full-employment level of real GDP. The recessionary gap (the difference between Yf and Y) is to be eliminated. The increase in spending shifts the aggregate demand curve AD from AD to AD1, and increases the equilibrium level of real GDP from Y to Yf, thus getting rid of the recession.

Scenario 73: A Matter of Crowding Out. Why an Increase in Government Spending Might Not Be Expansionary

Jim's assertion that an increase in government spending may not be expansionary is correct. We can consider just one case. Suppose the government borrows from consumers and firms (the private sector) in order to increase its spending. According to the loanable funds theory of interest, this increase in demand for loans will increase the rate of interest. Now, when the rate of interest rises, private sector spending will decrease and nullify (crowd out) the increase in government spending. It is for this reason that Jim is asserting that government spending may not be expansionary.

Scenario 74: A Peek at General Equilibrium Analysis: Raising the Bar

Hand-out on General Equilibrium Analysis

AN INTRODUCTION TO GENERAL EQUILIBRIUM ANALYSIS

The main purpose of this hand-out is to provide you with a general introduction to *General Equilibrium Analysis*. This is a very important tool that economists use to understand and explain certain economic phenomena.

Definition

General equilibrium analysis studies explicitly the interrelationships among various markets. In the real world in which we live and work, changes in one market cause repercussions in several other markets. This hand-out introduces you to general equilibrium analysis at a very rudimentary level.

Assumptions

To simplify the analysis, let us make the following assumptions about the economy of the country we shall call Newgen:

1. There are only two industries, namely, the apple industry and the bead industry.
2. The industries use only one factor of production: labour.
3. Labour resources are fully employed
4. The initial wage rate (that is, the price of labour) is the same in both industries.

The Analysis

Production Possibilities

Now, suppose that Newgen initially chooses to produce 50,000 pounds of apples and 150,000 beads. This combination of apples and beads is illustrated by point **A** on the production possibility curve shown below.

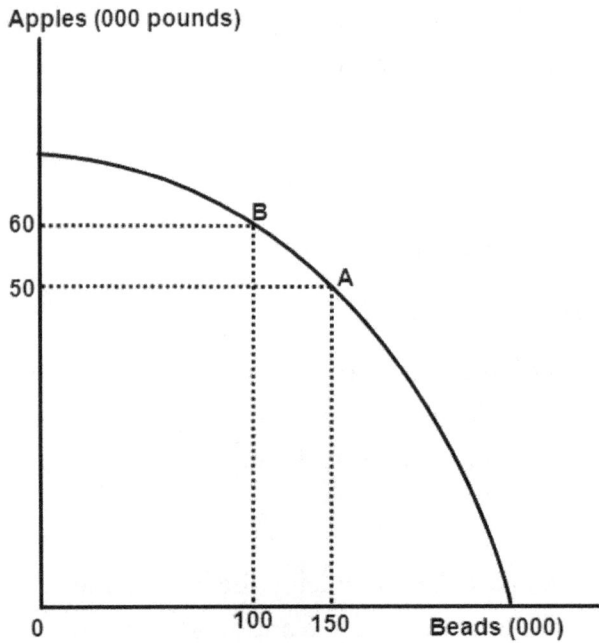

Apples (000 pounds)

60 ····· B

50 ····· A

0   100   150   Beads (000)

Product Market

If we assume that these are equilibrium quantities, we can show the initial market conditions for apples and beads in Figures A and B below respectively.

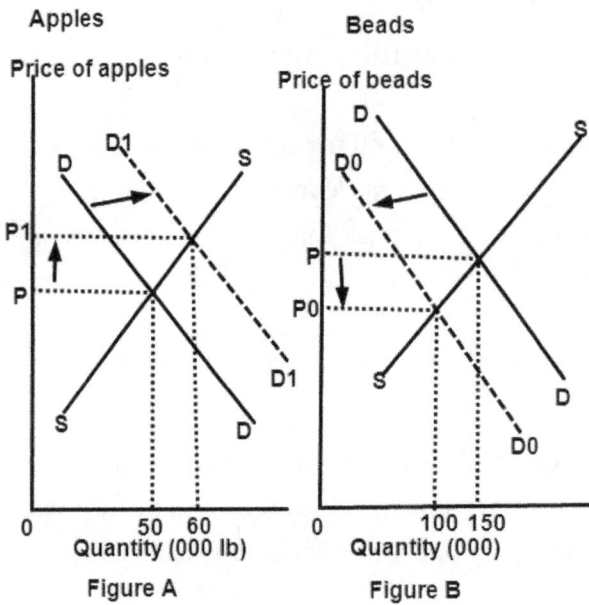

Apples

Price of apples

D1

D   S

P1 ·····

P ·····

S   D

D1

0   50 60
Quantity (000 lb)

Figure A

Beads

Price of beads

D

D0

S

P ·····

P0 ·····

S   D

D0

0   100 150
Quantity (000)

Figure B

204

Suppose now, that consumer tastes change in favour of more apples and fewer beads, as indicated by point B on the production possibility curve above. Figures A and B show respectively the increase in demand for apples and the fall in demand for beads. In Figure A, the increase in demand from DD to D1D1 results in an increase in the price of apples. In Figure B, the decrease in demand for beads from DD to D0D0 results in a fall in the price of beads.

Resource Market

Let us now investigate the resource or factor market. Figures C and D below show market conditions for labour resources. Figure C shows the demand for and supply of labour resources in the apple industry, and Figure D shows the demand for and supply of labour resources in the bead industry. The increase in demand for apples in the product market results in an increase in demand for labour in the apple industry—shown in Figure C as the change in demand for labour from DD to D1D1. This increased demand for labour, in turn, results in an increase in wages in the apple industry. The fall in the demand for beads causes demand for labour in the bead industry to decrease. Figure D shows this decrease as a shift in the demand for labour curve in the bead market from DD to D0D0. This decreased demand for labour causes wage rates to fall in the bead industry. If labour is substitutable between the two industries, workers will tend to move from the low-wage industry to the high-wage industry and bid the wage rate down. This movement will cease when the wage rate is again equal in both industries.

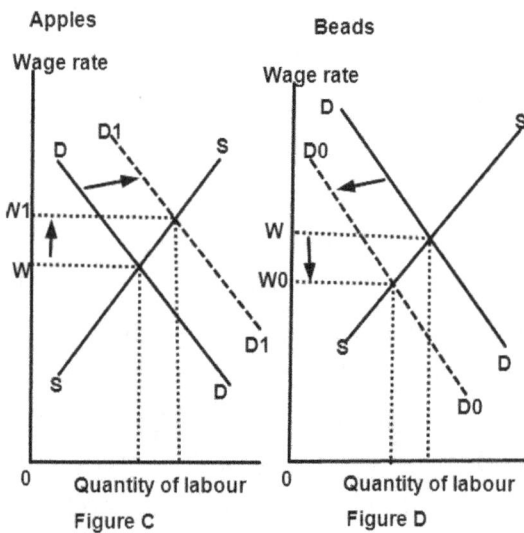

Figure C

Figure D

205

Conclusion

This general equilibrium analysis has enabled us to trace the effects of changes in product markets on factor markets. It points out the important fact that real-world markets are interrelated, not isolated.

Scenario 75: Can You Spot Them In There? Demand and Supply in the Circular Flow Model

The following diagram represents the circular flow model with a factor market (FM) and a product market (PM). The arrows indicate the direction of flow.

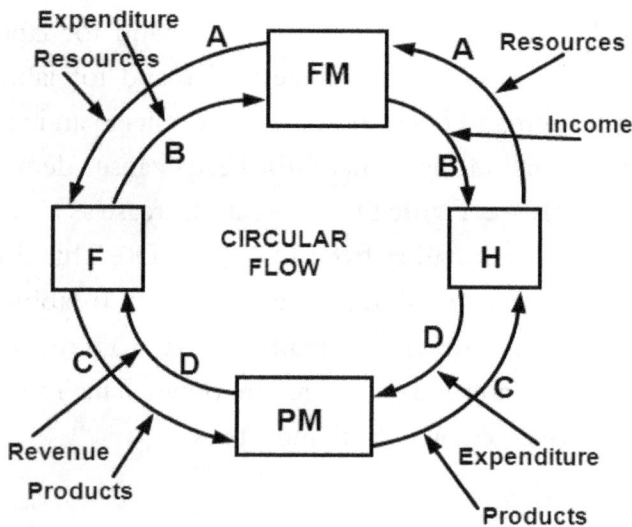

Let us begin with the *supply* of resources. This is indicated by flow **A** from the households to the factor market. This is the same flow from the factor market to the firms. The *demand* for resources is represented by flow **B** from the firms to the factor market. This is the same flow from the factor market to the households which they receive as income from the sale of their resources. The *supply* of products (goods and services) is represented by flow **C** from the firms to the product market. This is the same flow from the product market to the households. The *demand* for products is represented by flow **D** from the households to the product market. We have thus indicated the demand for and supply of resources *and* the demand for and supply of goods and services in the circular flow model.

Test 1

PART 1: DEFINITIONS (10 MARKS)

(a) Social science: Social science is any discipline that studies human behaviour. Examples of social science are economics, sociology, political science, and psychology

(b) Positive statement: A positive statement is a statement about facts and can be verified empirically. An example of a positive statement is: *six hundred students enrolled in economics this semester.*

(c) Rent: Rent is the income earned from land. If you hire out your private lake on the week-ends, the income thus earned is rent.

(d) Production possibility (p-p) schedule: A p-p schedule is a table that shows the various combinations of goods and services that an economy can produce if it uses all its resources and if technology is constant. The following is an example of a p-p schedule where Qa is the quantity of A and Qb is the quantity of B that the economy can produce.

Qa	Qb
0	6
1	4
2	2
3	0

(e) Product market: The product market, also called the *goods and services market*, is the market in which goods and services are exchanged. The market where one buys shoes is an example of a product market.

PART 2: MULTIPLE-CHOICE QUESTIONS (20 MARKS)

2b	3d	4d	5b	6d
7b	8c	9d	10b	11d
12c	13c	14c	15b	16a
17b	18c	19b	20a	21c

PART 3: PROBLEMS AND EXERCISES (5 MARKS)

22. Production-Possibility Curves

Legend: _____ = original, ----------- = new

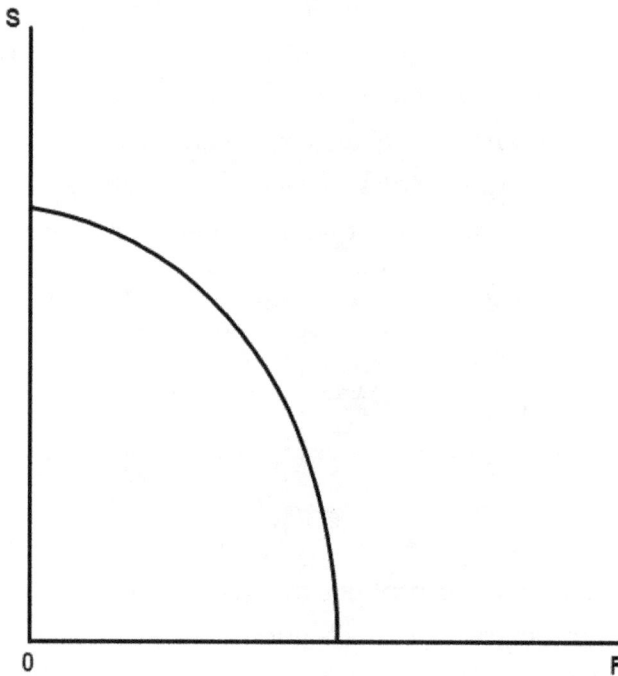

(a) A change in the prices of furniture and smart phones does not affect the economy's ability to produce these items; therefore the curve does not shift.

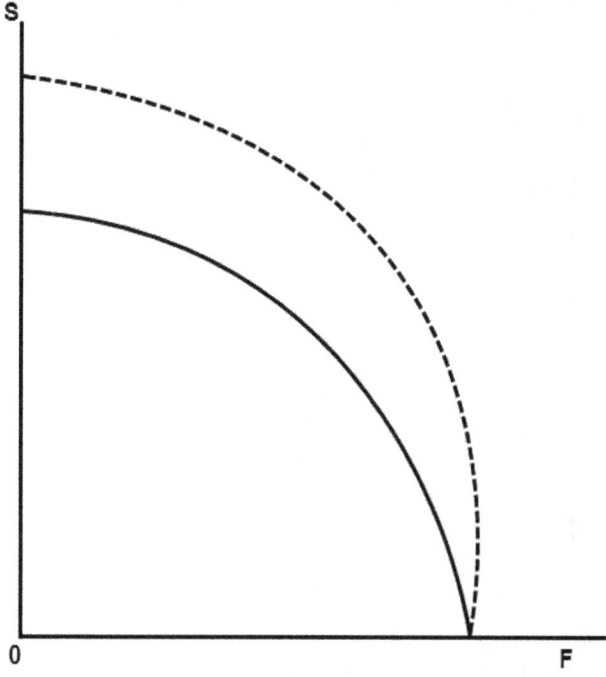

(b) This results in a non-parallel shift of the P-P curve as shown.

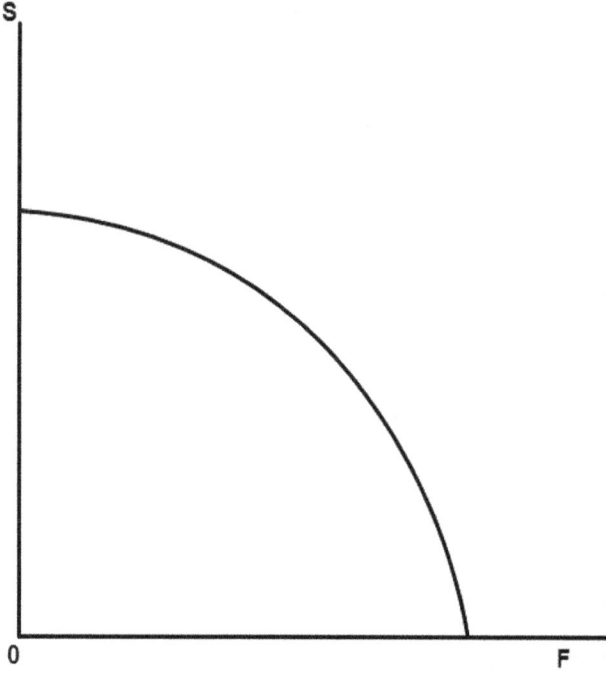

(c) The economy's productive capacity is not affected; therefore the P-P curve does not shift.

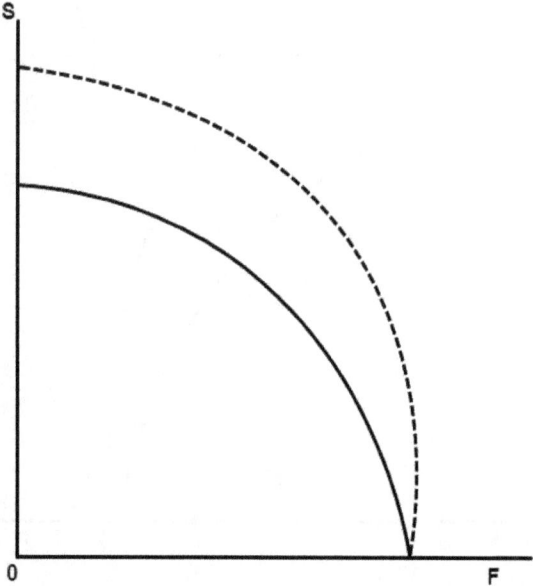

(d) The ability to produce smart phones has increased but there is no change in the ability to produce furniture. There is a non-parallel shift as shown.

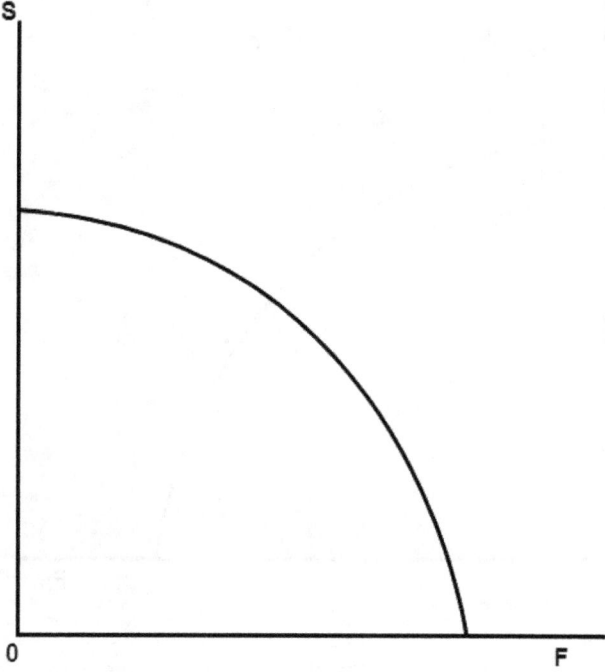

(e) There is no change in the economy's capacity to produce either smart phones or furniture; therefore the P-P curve does not shift.

PART 4: ESSAY QUESTION (5 MARKS)

23.

(f) An economic model is a simplification of a real economy or some aspect of it—an abstraction from reality—and it consists only of the factors that appear to pertain most to what is being studied. Details that do not pertain directly to the question or problem being studied are simply stripped away in the model.

(g) Economic models simplify economic reality. The real economy is extremely complex, much more so than is realized at first glance, and without models that reduce the complexities to manageable dimensions, economists (and those who study the economy) would not learn much about how a real economy functions. Through the construction and use of economic models, economists are able to get a much clearer understanding of economic processes and problems such as inflation, unemployment, economic growth, and business cycles.

Test 1A (Alternative)

PART 1: DEFINITIONS (10 MARKS)

1.

(h) Real capital: Real capital is any manufactured item that can be used to produce goods and services. Buildings, roads, manufacturing plants (factories), equipment, and tools are examples of real capital. Money is usually classified as financial capital.

(i) Flow: A flow (or a flow variable) is a measure of the change during a period of time. An example of a flow is a salary of $700 per week.

(j) Relative scarcity: Relative scarcity (also referred to as economic scarcity) refers to situations in which there are not enough resources to produce all the goods and services that would be necessary to satisfy all human wants.

(k) Endogenous variable: An endogenous variable is a variable whose value is determined within the model. For example, if we say that the quantity of tablets that people will buy depends on the price of tablets, then price would be an endogenous variable.

(l) Positive statement: A positive statement is an expression of how something is as opposed to how it ought to be. It is objective and based on facts. The following is an example of a positive statement: *Those who do a great deal of reading tend to get better grades in economics.*

PART 2: MULTIPLE-CHOICE QUESTIONS (20 MARKS)

2d	3c	4b	5d	6c
7b	8c	9d	10a	11b
12c	13d	14d	15b	16d
17a	18d	9d	20a	21d

PART 3: PROBLEMS AND EXERCISES (5 MARKS)

22. Production-Possibility Curve

Legend: _____ = original; ----------- = new

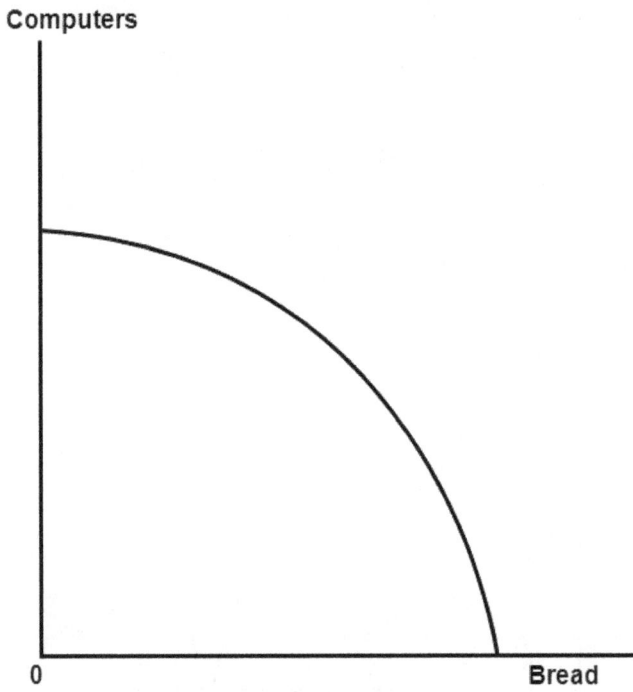

(a) The P-P curve remains the same but the actual production combination would change.

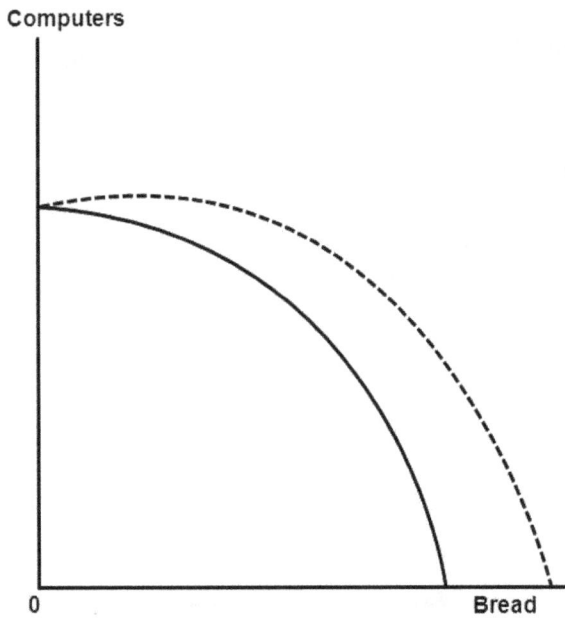

(b) The economy's ability to produce bread increases but its ability to produce computers is not affected. This results in a non-parallel shift in the P-P curve as shown.

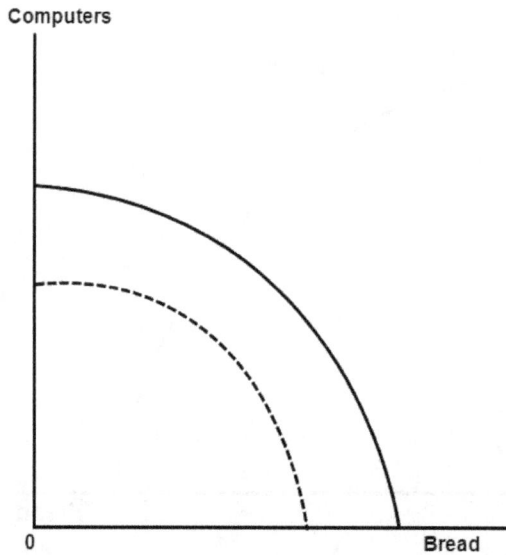

(c) The economy suffers a loss of resources; therefore, the P-P curve shifts to the left as shown.

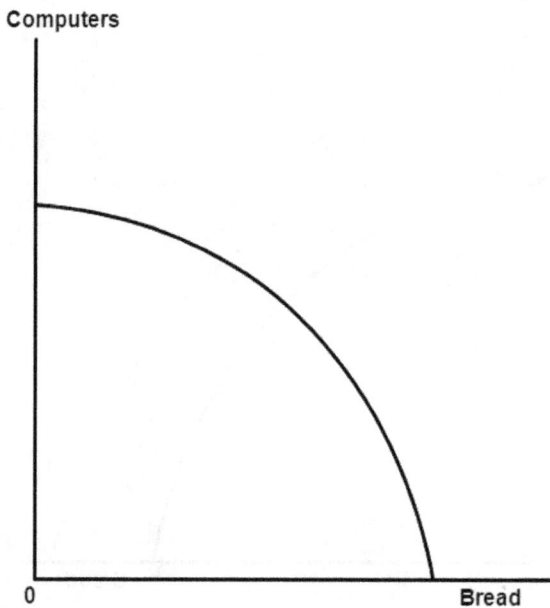

(d) The P-P curve does not shift because the economy's productive capacity is not affected.

Computers

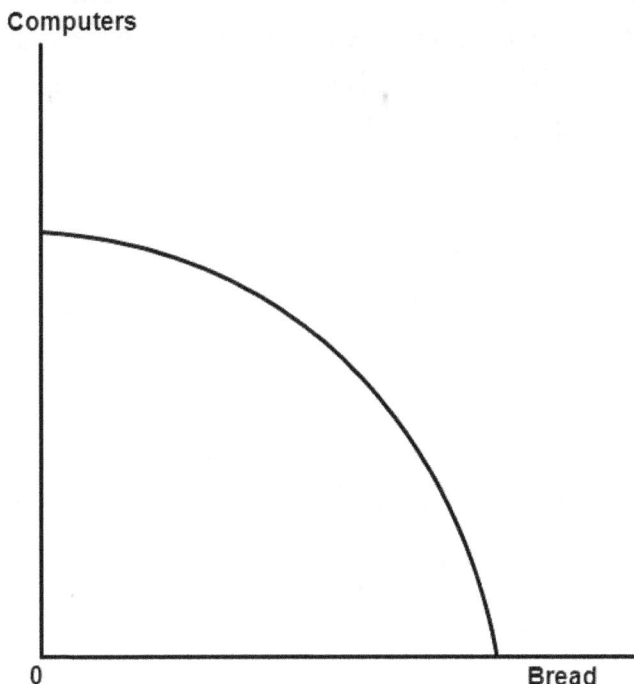

(e) There is no change in the P-P curve because the economy's ability to produce computers and bread is not affected.

PART 4: ESSAY QUESTION (5 MARKS)

23.

(m) An economic model is a hypothetical construct containing simplifying assumptions and hypotheses. Because the model is an abstraction from reality, it makes it easier to understand the relationships among economic variables. The model may be constructed using words, graphs, or mathematics.

(n) Economists construct models because it makes it easier for them to understand economic phenomena and processes, and thus helps them to get a clearer grasp of how the economy actually functions. Without the help of economic models, it would be much more difficult to understand the complexities of the real economy.

(o) One can determine the goodness of a model by how well it explains economic reality. The whole purpose of an economic model is to help us to explain some aspect of economic reality and to make predictions about economic outcomes. An economic model that does this well is a good model. If the model fails to explain economic reality, then it cannot be considered a good model.

Test 2

PART 1: DEFINITIONS (10 MARKS)

1.

(p) Supply curve: A supply curve is an upward sloping graph that shows the direct relationship between price and quantity supplied. The following diagram shows a supply curve.

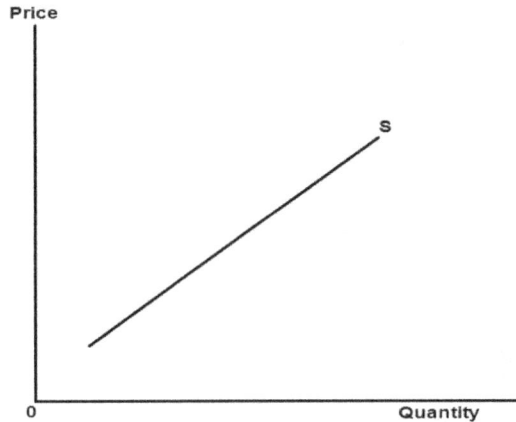

(q) Equilibrium price: Equilibrium price is the price at which quantity demanded and quantity supplied are equal. At that price, there is no tendency for the price to change because there is neither a shortage nor a surplus.

(r) Normal good: A normal good is a good or service such that as income increases, the demand for that good or service also increases. Most goods are normal goods.

(s) Intermediate product (in national income accounting): An intermediate product is an output of one firm or industry that is used as an input by another firm or industry. Intermediate products are usually intended to undergo further processing. Examples of intermediate products are steel, timber, plastic, and cotton.

(t) Net domestic income at factor cost (NDI): Net domestic income at factor cost is the sum of all incomes earned by the factors of production: wages and salaries + rent + interest and dividends + profits. It is one measure of total income.

PART 2. MULTIPLE-CHOICE (20 MARKS)

2a	3d	4b	5b	6a
7a	8c	9b	10b	11a
12b	13c	14d	15c	16c
17d	18c	19a	20a	21b

PART 3. PROBLEMS AND EXERCISES

22. Demand and Supply Graphs

Legend: _____ = original; ---------- = new

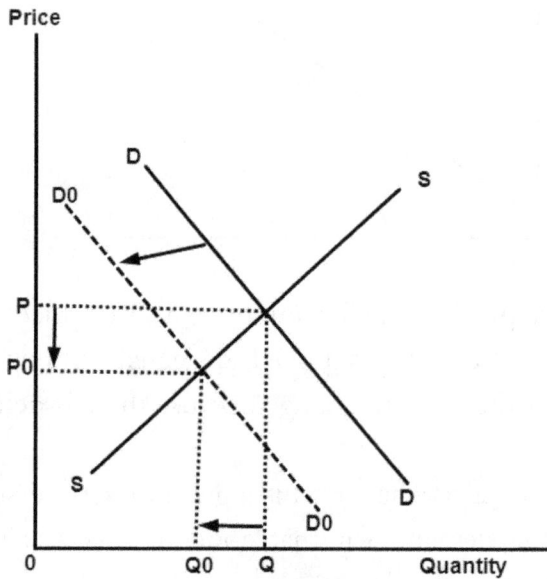

Price

D

D0

S

P

P0

S

D

D0

0   Q0   Q   Quantity

(a) A decrease in enrolment in colleges and universities will decrease the demand for reading lamps. The equilibrium price will fall and so will the equilibrium quantity.

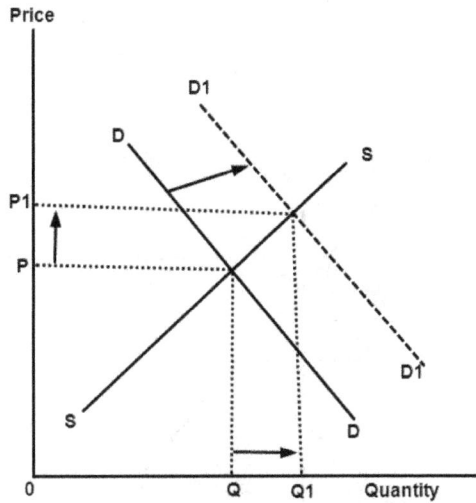

(b) The announcement that using reading lamps preserves vision will increase the demand for reading lamps, causing the equilibrium price and the equilibrium quantity of reading lamps to increase.

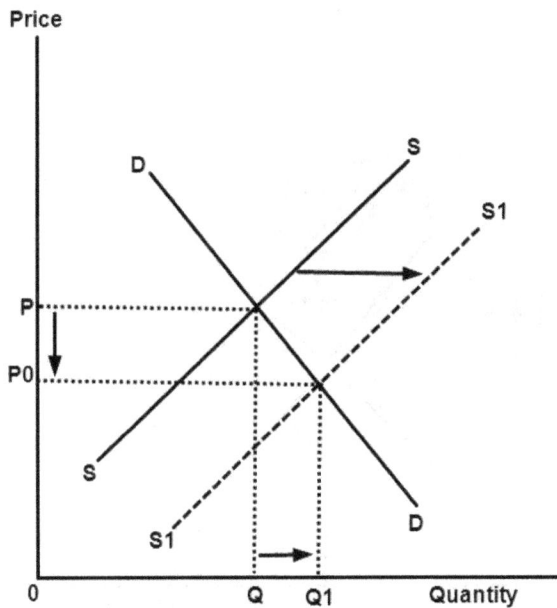

(c) A decrease in the cost of producing reading lamps will increase the supply of reading lamps. Consequently, the equilibrium price will fall, and the equilibrium quantity will increase.

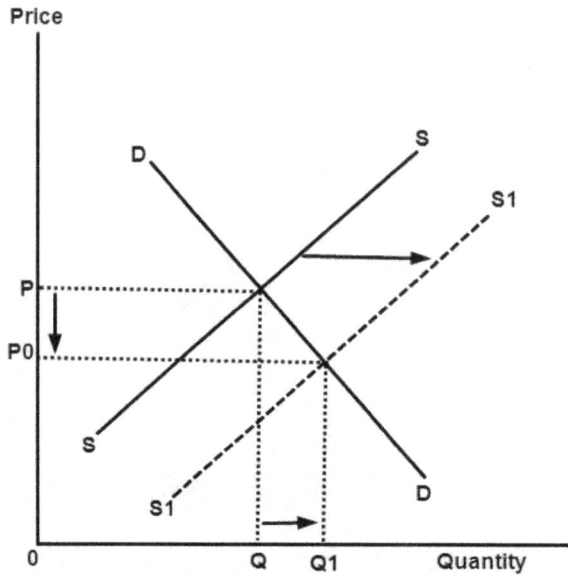

(d) A more efficient method of producing reading lamps will increase the supply of reading lamps. As a result, the equilibrium price will fall and the equilibrium quantity will increase.

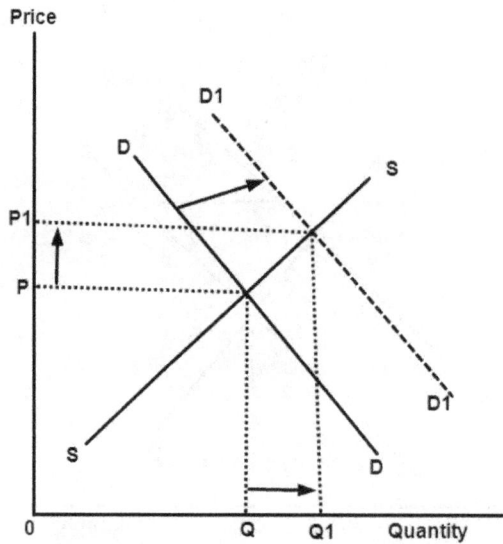

(e) Since reading lamps are considered to be normal goods, a general increase in income will increase the demand for reading lamps. This will result in an increase in the equilibrium price and an increase in the equilibrium quantity.

PART 4. ESSAY QUESTION (5 MARKS)

23. GDP suffers from a number of shortcomings when used as a measure of societal well-being. There are many things that give people enjoyment and satisfaction that are not included in the GDP measure. A few of these will be discussed here.

Leisure GDP does not measure the satisfaction and pleasure derived from leisure activities. Swimming in a pool, playing a game of cricket, enjoying a picnic at the beach, boating, skiing, bird watching, and playing a game of tennis all contribute to societal well-being, but they are not captured in the GDP measure.

Quality of life The quality of life may not be adequately reflected in GDP. People value security and a healthy environment. Most people, if given the choice, would prefer to live in a low-crime city than a crime-ridden one, other things being equal. They would also prefer to live in an environment with less pollution than one with more pollution.

Literacy Literacy is an important aspect of human well-being. A high level of literacy enables one to participate effectively in certain cultural and social activities from which much satisfaction can be obtained. Literacy also allows one to enjoy the benefits that participation in the democratic process can bring. Literacy gives access to a sea of information that can improve the well-being of people and their families. GDP does not measure this component of well-being.

Test 2A (Alternative)

PART 1: DEFINITIONS (10 MARKS)

1.

    a. Demand schedule: A demand schedule is a table that shows the various quantities of an item that people will be willing and able to buy at various prices during a period of time. The following table is an example of a demand schedule.

Price ($)	Quantity demanded
10	60
9	70
8	80
7	90

    b. Equilibrium quantity: The equilibrium quantity is the quantity that is demanded and supplied at the equilibrium price. It is the quantity at which the demand and supply curves intersect.

    c. Inferior good: An inferior good is a good for which the demand increases as income falls, and for which the demand falls as income rises. Used clothing is a good example of an inferior good.

    d. Double-counting (in national income accounting): Double-counting is the mistake of counting an item more than once. It occurs if an intermediate product is counted again in the final product. An example is counting plastic sold to a furniture manufacturer and counting it again in the plastic chair.

    e. The underground economy: The underground economy refers to all economic activities that are not reported to government and on which no taxes are paid; thus they are not reported in the national accounts. An example would be illegal prostitution.

PART 2: MULTIPLE-CHOICE (20 MARKS)

2d	3d	4d	5b	6d
7b	8d	9b	10a	11d
12a	13a	14d	15b	16d
17d	18d	19c	20d	21c

PART 3: PROBLEMS AND EXERCISES (5 MARKS)

22. Demand and Supply Graphs

Legend: _____ = original; ---------- = new

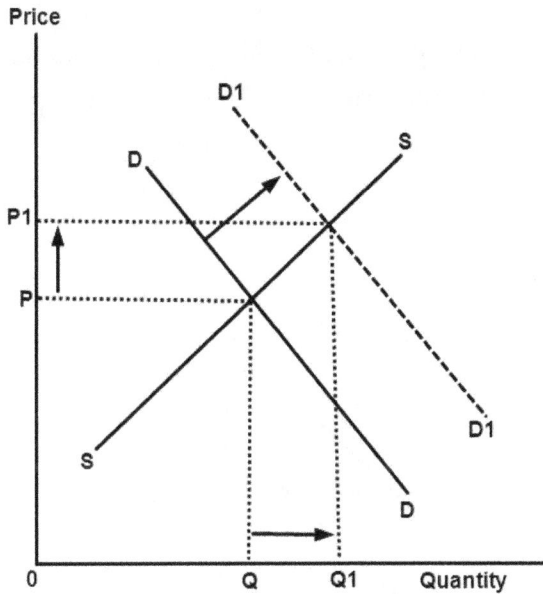

(a) This event will increase the demand for pencil cases. The demand curve will shift to the right, increasing both equilibrium price and equilibrium quantity.

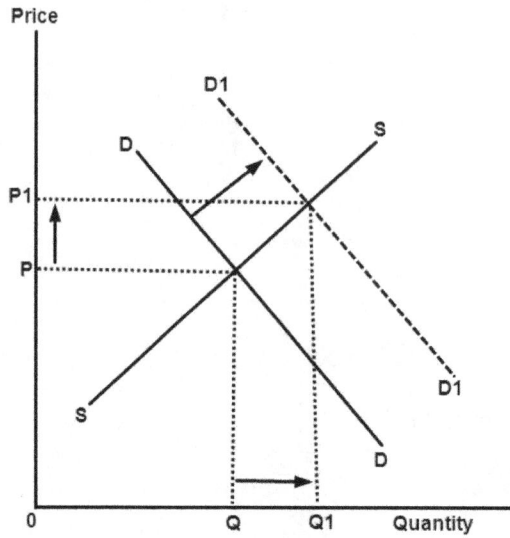

(b) An increase in the number of students will increase the demand for pencil cases. This will increase the equilibrium price and the equilibrium quantity.

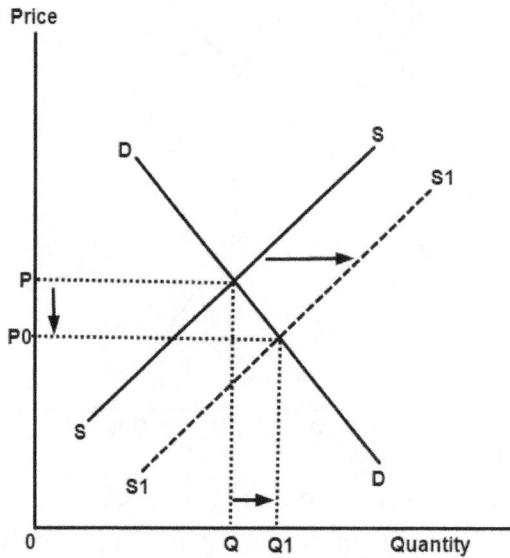

(c) An increase in the number of firms producing and selling pencil cases will increase the supply of pencil cases. As the supply curve shifts to the right, the equilibrium price falls and the equilibrium quantity increases.

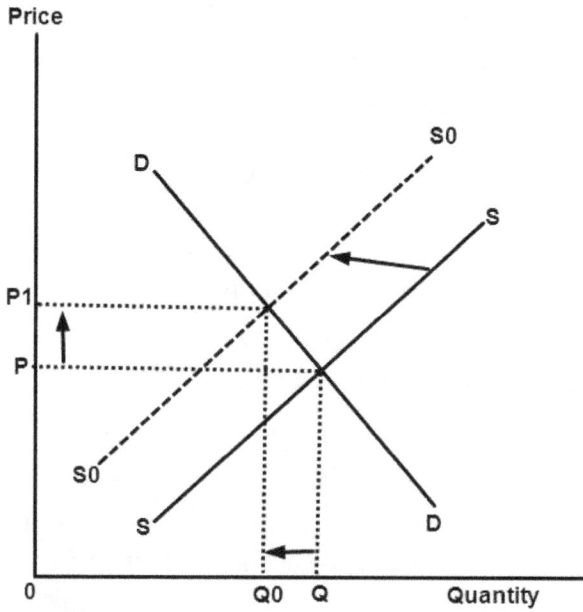

(d) An increase in the price of the material used to produce pencil cases will increase the cost of producing pencil cases and shift the supply curve to the left. This will result in an increase in the equilibrium price of pencil cases and a reduction in the equilibrium quantity.

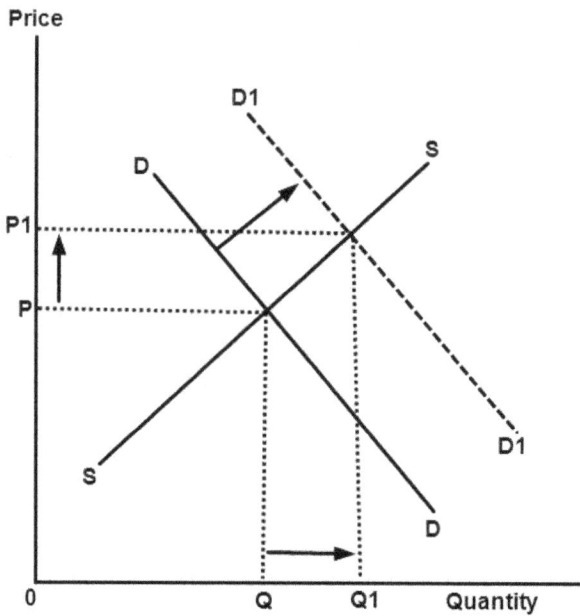

Pens and pencils are used with pencil cases. They are complementary goods to pencil cases. A decrease in the prices of pens and pencils will result in an increase in the quantity of pens and pencils demanded. Since people will have more pens and pencils, the demand for pencil cases will tend to increase, raising both the equilibrium price and the equilibrium quantity of pencil cases.

PART 4. ESSAY QUESTION (5 MARKS)

23. Gross domestic product (GDP) is the market value of all final goods and services produced within the borders of a country, regardless of who owns the resources used to produce the output. Gross national product (GNP) on the other hand, is the market value of all final goods and services produced by the country's resources, regardless of where the resources are located. Goods and services produced outside a country by its resources that are outside the country are a part of the country's GNP but not a part of its GDP. Goods and services produced within a country by foreign owned resources are a part of its GDP but not a part of its GNP.

Test 3

PART 1. DEFINITIONS (10 MARK)

1.

    f. Fiscal policy: Fiscal policy refers to changes in government spending and taxes

    g. Balanced budget: A balanced budget is a situation in which government spending equals its tax revenues

    h. Liquidity preference: Liquidity preference is the desire to hold money rather than less liquid interest-earning assets such as bonds.

    i. Marginal efficiency of investment: The marginal efficiency of investment is the expected return on additional investment. On a graph, it shows the inverse relationship between the rate of interest and the level of investment.

    j. Easy monetary policy: An easy monetary policy is an increase in the money supply and/or a reduction in interest rates by the central bank.

PART 2: MULTIPLE-CHOICE (20 MARKS)

2c	3c	4d	5c	6d
7d	8b	9b	10d	11c
12a	13b	14b	15c	16d
17b	18c	19d	20c	21d

PART 3. PROBLEMS AND EXERCISES (5 MARKS)

22.

Legend: _____ = original; ------------ = new

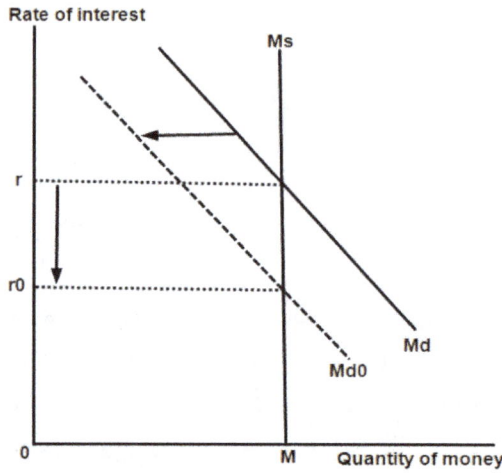

(a) The recession reduces income and thus decreases the demand for money. As a consequence, the equilibrium rate of interest falls, but equilibrium quantity of money remains the same.

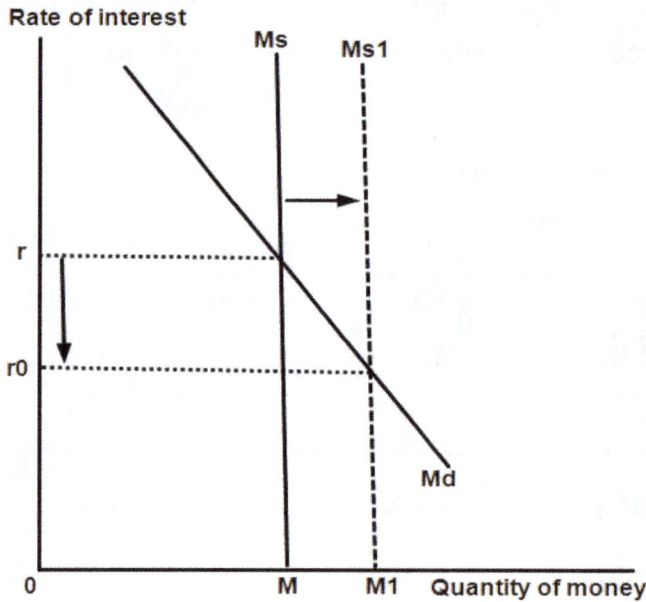

(b) An increase in the money supply shifts the money supply curve to the right, resulting in a fall in the equilibrium rate of interest and an increase in the equilibrium quantity of money.

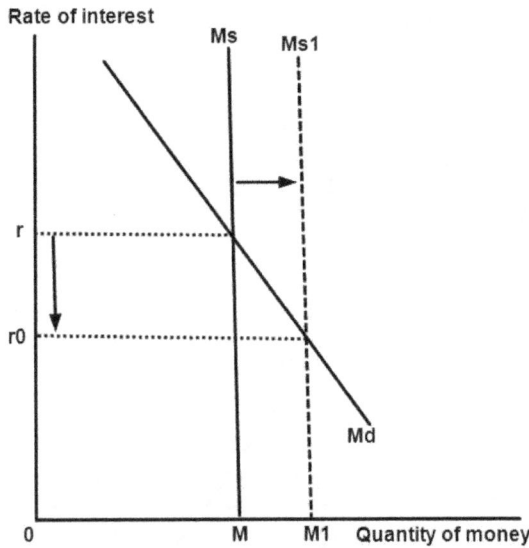

(c) An expansionary monetary policy shifts the money supply curve to the right, resulting in a fall in the equilibrium rate of interest and an increase in the equilibrium quantity of money.

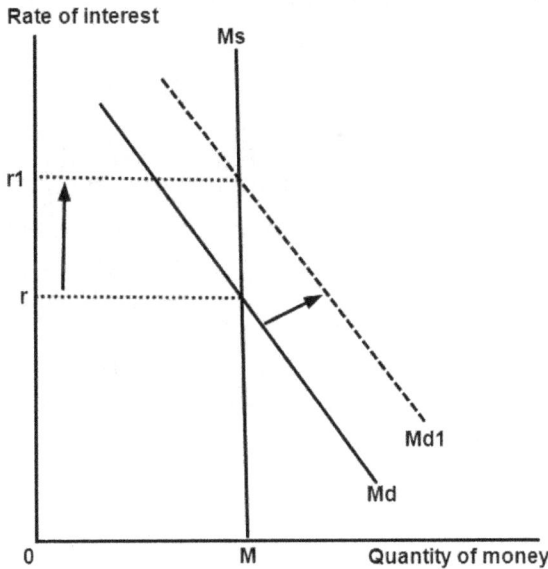

(d) An increase in wages is an increase in income that will increase the demand for money. Therefore, the demand curve sifts to the right, increasing the equilibrium rate of interest but leaving the equilibrium quantity of money unchanged.

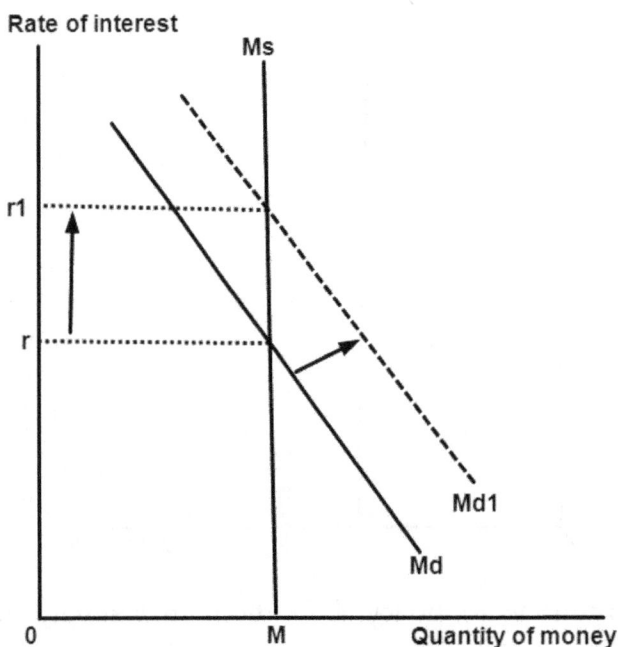

Rate of interest

Ms

r1

r

Md1

Md

0   M   Quantity of money

Both of these events will increase the demand for money and cause the demand curve to shift to the right. As a result, the equilibrium rate of interest will rise but the equilibrium quantity of money will not be affected.

PART 4. ESSAY (5 MARKS)

23. The appropriate advice to be given to the government is to implement a contractionary fiscal policy. In the following diagram, the economy is initially in equilibrium at full-employment with a price level of P which is inflationary. The desired price level is P0 which is consistent with full employment (yf). To reduce the price level, the aggregate demand (AD) curve must be shifted to the left to AD0. This can be accomplished by reducing government spending and increasing taxes.

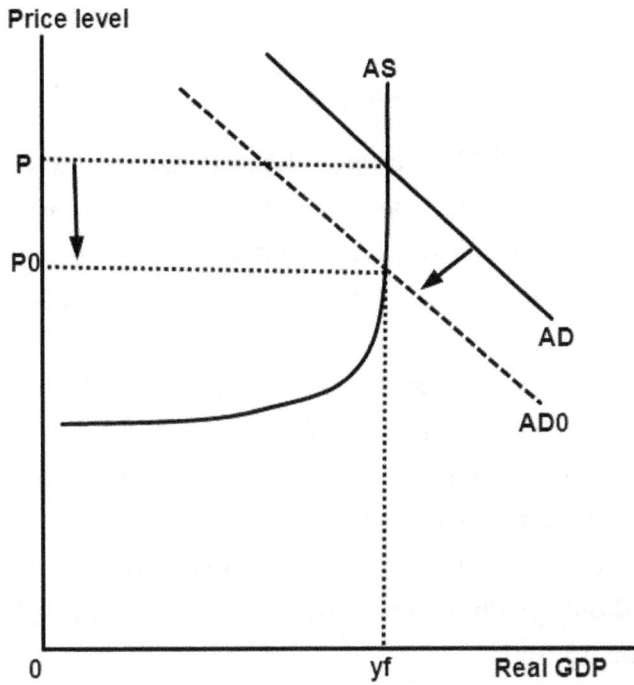

The appropriate advice to be given to the central bank is to implement a contractionary monetary policy. By reducing the money supply and raising interest rates, the AD curve will shift to the left as before, reducing the price level from P to P0. I would advise that these policies should be coordinated in order to avoid conflict.

Test 3A

PART 1. DEFINITIONS (10 MARKS)

a. Aggregate demand (AD) <u>curve:</u> The aggregate demand curve is a graph that shows the various quantities of all goods and services that will be demanded at various price levels during a period of time.

b. Keynesian range of the aggregate supply (AS) curve: The Keynesian range of the aggregate supply curve is the flat (horizontal) section of the curve that represents low output and high unemployment.

c. Budget surplus: A budget surplus is the condition that exists when government tax revenue exceeds government spending. A government budget surplus means that the government is saving.

d. Liquid asset: A liquid asset is an asset that can be easily converted into cash without much capital loss. An example of a liquid asset is a government bond.

e. Monetary policy: Monetary policy is action taken by a central bank to change interest rates and/or the quantity of money.

PART 2. MULTIPLE-CHOICE (20 MARKS)

2a	3c	4d	5a	6d
7a	8d	9b	10b	11c
12d	13b	14d	15c	16b
17c	18b	19c	20c	21b

PART 3. PROBLEMS AND EXERCISES (5 MARKS)

22. Legend: _____ = original; ------------ = new.

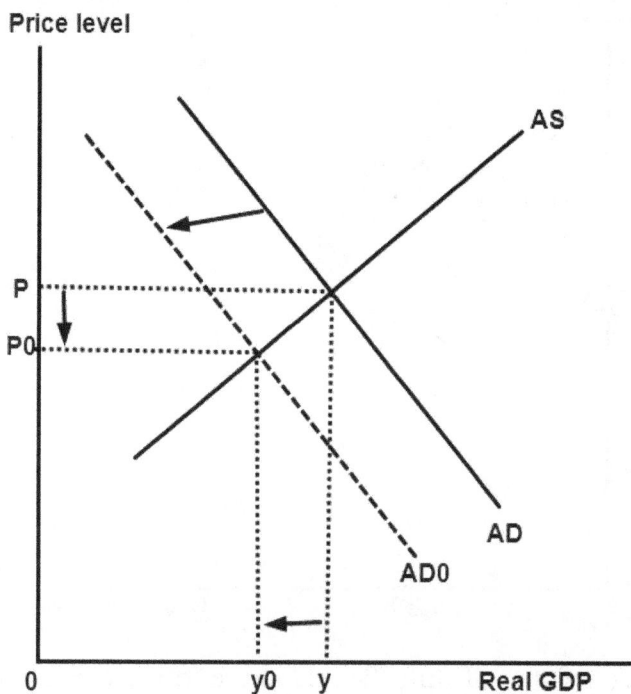

(a) A decrease in government spending will shift the AD curve to the left, resulting in a fall in the equilibrium price level and a fall in the equilibrium real GDP.

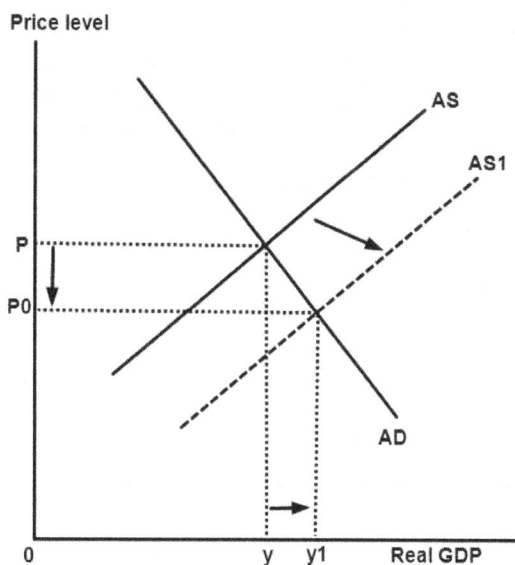

(b) A wave of new technology will shift the AS curve to the right, resulting in a fall in the equilibrium price level and an increase in equilibrium real GDP.

Price level

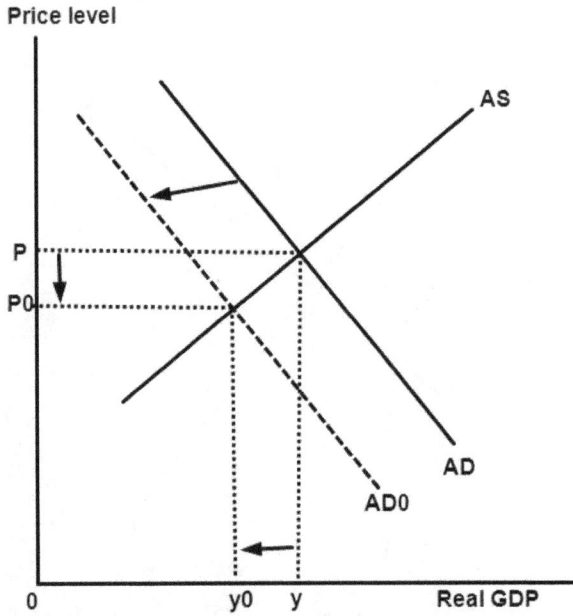

(c) A tight monetary policy will shift the AD curve to the left and reduce both the equilibrium price level and equilibrium real GDP.

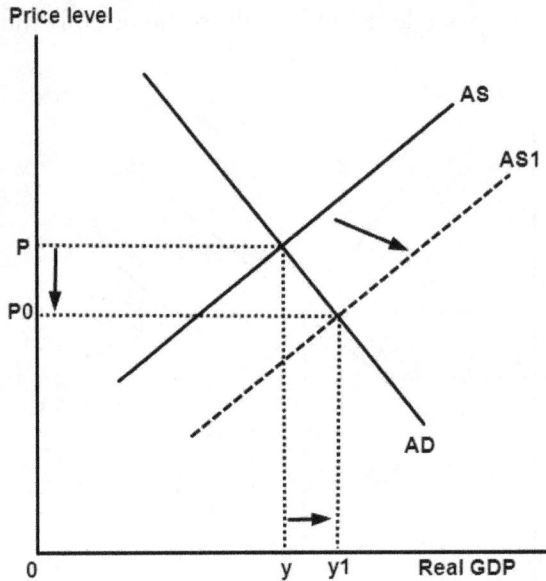

(d) A reduction in the cost of production will facilitate more production and thus shift the aggregate supply (AS) curve to the right. This will reduce the equilibrium price level and increase real GDP.

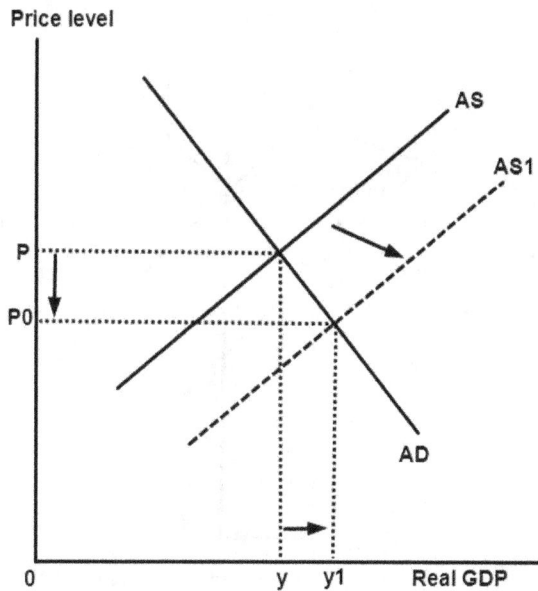

(e) Optimism on the part of consumers will cause them to increase their purchases of goods and services. This will shift the AD curve to the right, increasing the equilibrium price level and also increasing the equilibrium real GDP.

PART 4. ESSAY (5 MARKS)

23. The advice would pertain to fiscal policy since it's the government that will implement the policy. The problem here is that the economy is in equilibrium at a level of income that is significantly below the full-employment level. Such a situation is illustrated by a level of income of y and a price level of P in the diagram below.

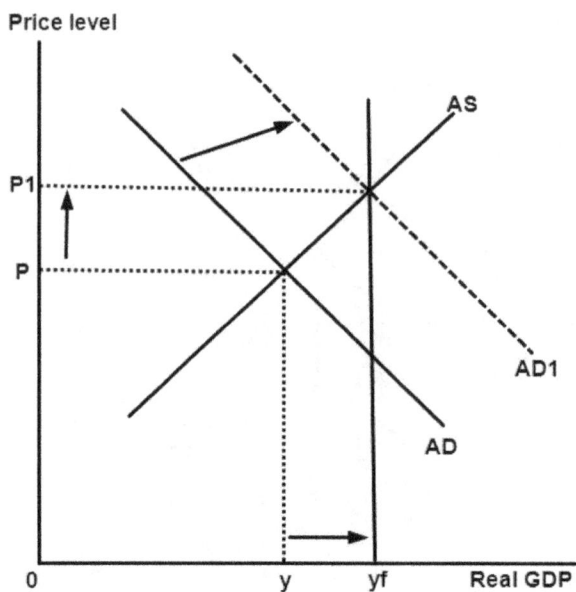

What is required is an increase in aggregate demand (AD) from AD to AD1 where the economy will be at full-employment equilibrium at yf and a price level of P1. This can be accomplished by an expansionary fiscal policy. The government can increase its spending and/or reduce taxes and thus accomplish this objective.